Whatever Happened to the Human Race?

" I'M GOING TO TAKE A NAP... WATCH MY PLUGS, WILL YOU? "

By **Francis A. Schaeffer**
The God Who Is There
Escape From Reason
He Is There and He Is Not Silent
Death in the City
Pollution and the Death of Man
The Church at the End of the 20th Century
The Mark of the Christian
The Church Before the Watching World
True Spirituality
Basic Bible Studies
Genesis in Space and Time
The New Super-Spirituality
Back to Freedom and Dignity
Art and the Bible
No Little People
Two Contents, Two Realities
Joshua and the Flow of Biblical History
No Final Conflict
Everybody Can Know (with *Edith Schaeffer*)
How Should We Then Live?
Whatever Happened to the Human Race?
      (with *C. Everett Koop, M.D.*)
A Christian Manifesto

By **C. Everett Koop, M.D.**
Scientific monographs, textbook chapters, and papers on the general
fields of pediatric surgery, nutritional research, biomedical ethics.

The Right to Live; The Right to Die
Whatever Happened to the Human Race?
      (with *Francis A. Schaeffer*)

Whatever Happened to the Human Race?

Revised Edition

C. Everett Koop, M.D.
Francis A. Schaeffer

CROSSWAY BOOKS • WESTCHESTER, ILLINOIS
A DIVISION OF GOOD NEWS PUBLISHERS

Whatever Happened to the Human Race? has also been made into a major film series, available for rent from Gospel Films, Inc., Muskegon, Michigan, 1-800-253-0413. Produced by Franky Schaeffer, it is a comprehensive presentation of the ideas developed in this book. The text and narration are by C. Everett Koop and Francis A. Schaeffer.

Scripture quotations not otherwise identified are from HOLY BIBLE New International Version, copyright © 1978 New York International Bible Society. Used by permission.

Excerpt from "Medical Science Under Dictatorship" by Leo Alexander is reprinted by permission from *The New England Journal of Medicine* (241:39–47, July 14, 1949).

Excerpt from "No-Fault Guilt-Free History" by Dr. Richard M. Hunt is from *The New York Times,* February 16, 1976. Copyright © 1976 by The New York Times Company. Used by permission.

Excerpt entitled "You Be the Judge" is used by permission of the publisher of *National Newsline,* Nurses Concerned for Life, Inc.

To those who were robbed of life, the unborn, the weak, the sick, the old, during the dark ages of madness, selfishness, lust and greed for which the last decades of the twentieth century are remembered.

Contents

Preface

Unimaginable events are taking place in our world today. What was once unthinkable has become thinkable—and is actually happening.

● In 1982 over 1.6 million unborn children were killed inside their mother's womb in America. In one case a prominent New York doctor inserted a needle into the heart of one unborn twin boy and withdrew enough of the child's blood to kill him. The baby's mother had learned that one of her twins was handicapped. She wanted only the "perfect child" to live. The case was hailed as a medical milestone by many physicians.

● In that same year a newborn baby boy was starved to death in a Bloomington, Indiana hospital. It was a clear-cut case of infanticide. This baby was also handicapped (although not severely so), and his parents reasoned that death by starvation was better than life with a handicap. Several doctors and lawyers have even suggested that we have a waiting period of several days for all newborn infants before we certify them "truly human." We could then kill "imperfect" children during the first days of life with no penalty under the law.

● In England a death pill for the aged has been introduced. Doctors are predicting it will be available and perhaps mandatory by the end of this century. In Sweden one doctor wants to open a "suicide clinic" to help fellow Swedes learn how to kill themselves more effectively.

We are witnessing the devaluation and destruction of innocent human lives on a massive scale.

We ask ourselves how this has happened. How is it that we have arrived at the point in our society where we can abort 1.6 million unborn children and leave some of our handicapped babies to die in hospital nurseries? We confess that often we do not fully understand. We are left with only the bits and pieces of these issues as they appear on television and radio. We cannot see the causes and consequences of what is happening around us.

But events do not happen in a vacuum. Ideas have consequences, and abortion, infanticide, and euthanasia are the logical consequences of several powerful ideas. We are told that man is not accountable to God and that we can remake man in our own image. Many believe that some human lives are not worth protecting and that human beings must measure up to certain standards before they can be members of the human family.

These ideas have taken root in American society. They have brought with them the devaluation and destruction of many innocent human lives. To understand these life issues we must understand the ideas behind them and their power and presence with us today.

Our understanding and action are crucial. Every age has its moral issues that define it, and determine if history will look back and say that this was a noble and compassionate age or one of tyranny and inhumanity. The human life issues will define our own time. For far from being only single issues, abortion, infanticide, and euthanasia strike at the heart of our most basic beliefs about God and man.

The way in which we ultimately decide them will determine the future for all of us. As Mother Teresa has said, "If a mother can kill her own children, then what can be next?" Indeed, what can be next for all of us? If we can take one life because it does not measure up to our standards of perfection, what is to stop us from taking any life—simply for our own convenience? Abortion and infanticide are only the beginning steps on a slippery slope that will lead to death for all but the planned and perfect members of our society.

These issues are a watershed for us. We must act now to protect the sanctity of every human life—a life that has been created in the image of God.

Whatever Happened to the Human Race? provides us with a foundation for understanding and action. We see not only the facts of abortion, infanticide, and euthanasia, but also the ideas behind these life and death issues. Dr. Schaeffer and Dr. Koop illuminate for us the anti-God and anti-life attitudes that dominate our society today. In these pages we find the tools for action to change what is happening in America. We find the answers we need to restore the dignity and sanctity of every stage of life.

The Publisher
June 1983

Just imagine that these events were to become known to the enemy! And were being exploited by them! In all probability, such propaganda would be ineffective simply because those hearing and reading it would not be prepared to believe it.

The Reichskommisar for the Ostland
to the Reichminister for occupied
Eastern territories—June 18, 1943

CHAPTER ONE

The Abortion of the Human Race

Cultures can be judged in many ways, but eventually every nation in every age must be judged by this test: *how did it treat people?* Each generation, each wave of humanity, evaluates its predecessors on this basis. The final measure of mankind's humanity is how humanely people treat one another.

The great dramatic moments of history have left us with monuments and memories of compassion, love, and unselfishness which punctuate the all-too-pervasive malevolence that dominates so much human interaction. That there is any respite from evil is due to some courageous people who, on the basis of personal philosophies, have led campaigns against the ill-treatment and misuse of individuals. Each era faces its own unique blend of problems. Our own time is no exception. Those who regard individuals as expendable raw material—to be molded, exploited, and then discarded—do battle on many fronts with those who see each person as unique and special, worthwhile, and irreplaceable.

The reason we are writing this book is that we feel strongly that we stand today on the edge of a great abyss. At this crucial moment choices are being made and thrust on us that will for many years to come affect the way people are treated. We want to try to help tip the scales on the side of those who believe that individuals are unique and special and have great dignity.

Yad Vashem is the monument in Jerusalem to the six million Jews and others who were killed in the Nazi Holocaust.[1] It is one of the many memorials that are scattered over the world in tribute to those who have perished in upheavals of rampant evil—evil that swirls in on people when they no longer have a basis for regarding one another as wonderful creatures worthy of special care. Yad Vashem is a fitting place to begin, for it reminds us of what, unhappily, is possible in human behavior. Those who were murdered were people just like all of us. More important to realize is that those who murdered them were also people just like all of us. We seem to be in danger of forgetting our seemingly unlimited capacities for evil, once boundaries to certain behavior are removed.

There are choices to be made in every age. And who we are depends on the choices we make. What will our choices be? What boundaries will we uphold to make it possible for people to say with certainty that moral atrocities are truly evil? Which side will we be on?

The Thinkable and the Unthinkable

There is a "thinkable" and an "unthinkable" in every era. One era is quite certain intellectually and emotionally about what is acceptable. Yet another era decides that these "certainties" are unacceptable and puts another set of values into practice. On a humanistic base, people drift along from generation to generation, and the morally unthinkable becomes the thinkable as the years move on. By "humanistic base" we mean the fundamental idea that men and women can begin from themselves and derive the standards by which to judge all matters. There are for such people no fixed standards of behavior, no standards that cannot be eroded or replaced by what seems necessary, expedient, or even fashionable.

Perhaps the most striking and unusual feature of our moment of history is the speed with which eras change. Looking back in history, we notice that cultures such as the Indus River civilization (the Harappa culture) lasted about a thousand years. Today the passing of eras is so greatly speeded up that the 1960s stand in sharp contrast to the 1970s. The young people of the seventies do not understand their older brothers and sisters of the sixties. What was unthinkable in the sixties is unthinkable no longer.

The ease and speed of communication has been a factor in this. A protest in South Africa, for example, can be echoed by sympathizers in New York in just a few hours. Social conventions appear and disappear with unprecedented rapidity.

The thinkables of the eighties and nineties will certainly include things which most people today find unthinkable and immoral, even unimaginable and too extreme to suggest. Yet—since they do not have some overriding principle that takes them beyond relativistic thinking—when these become thinkable and acceptable in the eighties and nineties, most people will not even remember that they were unthinkable in the seventies. They will slide into each new thinkable without a jolt.

What we regard as thinkable and unthinkable about how we treat human life has changed drastically in the West. For centuries Western culture has regarded human life and the quality of the life of the individual as special. It has been common to speak of "the sanctity of human life."

For instance, the Hippocratic Oath, which goes back more than 2,000 years, has traditionally been taken by the graduates of American medical schools at the time of their commencement.[2] The Declaration of Geneva (adopted in September 1948 by the General Assembly of the World Medical Organization and modeled closely on the Hippocratic Oath) became used as the graduation oath by more and more medical schools. It includes: "I will maintain the utmost respect for human life from the time of conception." This concept of the preservation of human life has been the basis of the medical profession and society in general. It is significant that when the University of Pittsburgh changed from the Hippocratic Oath to the Declaration of Geneva in 1971, the students deleted "from the time of conception" from the clause beginning: "I will maintain the utmost respect for human life." The University of Toronto School of Medicine has also removed the phrase "from the time of conception" from the form of the oath it now uses.[3]

Of course, the Hippocratic Oath takes us back to the time of the Greeks. But the fully developed concept of the sanctity of human life that we have known did not come from Greek thought and culture but from the Judeo-Christian world-view which dominated the West for centuries. This view did *not* come from *nowhere*. Biblical doctrine was preached not as *a* truth but as *the* truth. This teaching formed not only the religious base of society but the cultural, legal, and governmental bases as well. As a total world-view it answered the major questions people have always asked. It dealt not only with the questions *Who is God? What is He like?* It also gave answers to the questions of *Who are we as people? How ought we to live together? What meaning does human life have?* In this way, Judeo-Christianity formed a general cultural consensus. That is, it provided the basic moral and social values by which things were judged.

Judeo-Christian teaching was never perfectly applied, but it did lay a foundation for a high view of human life in concept and practice. Knowing biblical values, people viewed human life as unique—to be protected and loved—because each individual is created in the image of God. This stands in great contrast, for example, to Roman culture. The Roman world practiced both abortion and infanticide, while Christian societies have considered abortion and infanticide to be murder.

Until recently in our own century, with some notable and sorry exceptions, human beings have generally been regarded as special, unique, and nonexpendable. But in one short generation we have moved from a generally high view of life to a very low one.

Why has our society changed? The answer is clear: the consensus of our society no longer rests on a Judeo-Christian base, but rather on a humanistic one. Humanism makes man "the measure of all things." It puts man rather than God at the center of all things.

Today the view that man is a product of chance in an impersonal universe dominates both sides of the Iron Curtain. This has resulted in a secularized society and in a liberal theology in much of the church; that is, the Bible is set aside and humanism in some form (man starting from himself) is put in the Bible's place. Much of the church no longer holds that the Bible is God's Word in all it teaches. It simply blends with the current thought-forms rather than being the "salt" that judges and preserves the life of its culture. Unhappily, this portion of the church simply changes its standards as the secular, humanist standards sweep on from one loss of humanness to the next. What we are watching is the natural result of humanism in its secular and theological forms, and the human race is being increasingly devalued.

In our time, humanism has replaced Christianity as the consensus of the West. This has had many results, not the least of which is to change people's view of themselves and their attitudes toward other human beings. Here is how the change came about. Having rejected God, humanistic scientists, philosophers and professors began to teach that only what can be mathematically measured is real and that all reality is like a machine. Man is only one part of the larger cosmic machine. Man is more complicated than the machines people make, but is still a machine, nevertheless.

As an example, in 1968 Dr. Edmund R. Leach, Provost of Kings College, Cambridge, wrote in the *London Times:*

> Today when the molecular biologists are rapidly unravelling the genetic chemistry of all living things—while the radio astronomers are deciphering the programme of an evolving cosmos—all the marvels of creation are seen to be mechanisms rather than mysteries. Since even the human brain is nothing more than an immensely complicated computer, it is no longer necessary to invoke metaphysics to explain how it works. In the resulting mechanistic universe all that remains of the divine will is the moral consciousness of man himself.

How unsatisfactory this evaluation is can be seen in the fact that a decade later every point Edmund Leach made is still in question.

Nonetheless, even though the years pass and men like Leach do not prove their points, the idea of a purely mechanistic universe with people as only complicated machines infiltrates the thinking of many. By constant repetition, the idea that man is nothing more than a machine has captured the popular mind. This idea keeps being presented year after year in the schools and in the media, however unfounded and unproven the hypothesis. Gradually, after being generally unquestioned, it is blindly accepted— just as, after many years of teaching that the earth was flat, the notion was believed because of its sheer pervasiveness. Flawed and erroneous teachings about mankind, however, have far more serious effects. After all, they are talking about *us*.

For a while, Western culture—from sheer inertia—continued to live by the old Christian ethics while increasingly embracing the mechanistic, time-plus-chance view of people. People came more and more to hold that the universe is intrinsically and originally impersonal—as a stone is impersonal. Thus, *by chance,* life began on the earth and then, through long, long periods of time, *by chance,* life became more complex, until man with his special brain came into existence. By "chance" is meant that there was no reason for these things to occur; they just happened that way. No matter how loftily it is phrased, this view drastically reduces our view of self-worth as well as our estimation of the worth of others, for we are viewing ourselves as mere accidents of the universe.

Sociological Law and Personal Cruelty
Recently a generation has arisen that has taken these theories out of the lab and classroom and into the streets. Its members have carried the reduction of the value of human beings into everyday life. Suddenly we find ourselves in a more consistent but uglier world—more consistent because people are taking their low view of man to its natural conclusion, and uglier because humanity is drastically dehumanized.

To illustrate what it means to practice this low view of man, let us consider some present realities that only a few years ago would have been unthinkable—even on the base provided by a memory of the Christian consensus, let alone within the Christian consensus itself. The Christian consensus gave a basis and a framework for our society to have freedoms without those freedoms leading to chaos. There was an emphasis on the value of the individual person—whose moral choices proceed from judgments about man and society on the basis of the existence of the infinite-personal God and His teaching in the Bible.

The Bible teaches that man is made in the image of God and therefore is unique. Remove that teaching, as humanism has done on both sides of the Iron Curtain, and there is no adequate basis for treating people well. Let us now look at some of those related unthinkable realities. The loss of the Christian consensus has led to a long list of inhuman actions and attitudes which may seem unrelated but actually are not. They are the direct result of the loss of the Christian consensus.

First, the whole concept of law has changed. When a Christian consensus existed, it gave a base for law. Instead of this, we now live under arbitrary, or sociological, law. Supreme Court Justice Oliver Wendell Holmes took a big step in the change toward sociological law. Holmes said, "Truth is the majority vote of that nation that could lick all others." In other words, law is only what most of the people think at that moment of history, and there is no higher law. It follows, of course, that the law can be changed at any moment to reflect what the majority currently thinks.

More accurately, the law becomes what a few people in some branch of the government think will promote the present sociological and economic good. In reality the will and moral judgments of the majority are now influenced by or even overruled by the opinions of a small group of men and women. This means that vast changes can be made in the whole concept of what should and what should not be done. Values can be altered overnight and at almost unbelievable speed.

Consider the influence of the United States Supreme Court. Ralph Winter, reviewing *The Memoirs of Earl Warren,* said in the *Wall Street Journal* of July 27, 1977, that a large body of academic criticism has argued that the Warren Court was essentially anti-democratic because it paid little heed to traditional legal criteria and procedures and rewrote law according to the personal values of its members. Winter summed up Supreme Court Justice Douglas's concept as, "If the Supreme Court does it, it's all right." The late Alexander M. Bickel of Yale said that the Supreme Court was undertaking "to bespeak the people's general will when the vote comes out wrong." And Bickel caustically summed the matter up by saying, "In effect, we must now amend the Constitution to make it mean what the Supreme Court says it means."[4]

The shift to *sociological* law can affect everything in life, including who should live and who should die.

Those taking the lead in the changes involving who should live and who should die increasingly rely on litigation (the courts) rather than legislation and the election process. They do this because they can often accomplish through the courts changes they could not achieve by the will of the majority, using the more representative institutions of government.

The Christian consensus held that neither the majority nor an elite is absolute. God gives the standards of value, and His absolutes are binding on both the ordinary person and those in all places of authority.

Second, because the Christian consensus has been put aside, we are faced today with a flood of personal cruelty. As we have noted, the Christian consensus gave great freedoms without leading to chaos—because society in general functioned within the values given in the Bible, especially the unique value of human life. Now that humanism has taken over, the former freedoms run riot, and individuals, acting on what they are taught, increasingly practice their cruelties without restraint. And why shouldn't they? If the modern humanistic view of man is correct and man is only a product of chance in a universe that has no ultimate values, why should an individual refrain from being cruel to another person, if that person seems to be standing in his or her way?

Abusing Genetic Knowledge
Beyond the individual's cruelty to other individuals, why should society not make over humanity into something different if it can do so—even if it results in the loss of those factors which make human life worth living? New genetic knowledge could be used in a helpful way and undoubtedly will bring forth many things which are beneficial, but—once the uniqueness of people as created by God is removed and mankind is viewed as only one of the gene patterns which came forth on the earth by chance—there is no reason not to treat people as things to be experimented on and to make over the whole of humanity according to the decisions of a relatively few individuals. If people are not unique, as made in the image of God, the barrier is gone. Once this barrier is gone there is no reason not to experiment genetically with humanity to make it into what someone thinks to be an improvement socially and economically. The cost here is overwhelming. Should the genetic changes once be made in the individual, these changes will be passed down to his or her children, and they cannot ever be reversed.

Modern humanism has an inherent need to manipulate and tinker with the natural processes, including human nature, because humanism:

1. Rejects the doctrine of Creation.
2. Therefore rejects the idea that there is anything stable or "given" about human nature.
3. Sees human nature as part of a long, unfolding process of development in which everything is changing.
4. Casts around for some solution to the problem of despair that this determinist-evolutionist vision induces.
5. Can only find a solution in the activity of the human will, which—in opposition to its own system—it hopes can transcend the inexorable flow of nature and act upon nature.
6. Therefore encourages manipulation of nature, including tinkering with people, as the only way of escaping from nature's bondage. But this manipulation cannot have any certain criteria to guide it because, with God abolished, the only remaining criterion is nature (which is precisely what humanist man wants to escape from) and nature is both noncruel and cruel.

This explains why humanism is fascinated with the manipulation of human nature.

It is not only Christians who are opposed to the forms of genetic engineering which tinker with the structure of humanity. Others such as Theodore Roszak and Jeremy Rifkin of the People's Business Commission rightly see this genetic engineering as incompatible with democracy. Christians and other such people can raise their voices together against this threat. That does not, however, change the realization that the democracy such people are trying to save is a product of Reformation Christianity, and without Reformation Christianity the base for that democracy and its freedom is gone.

In sociological law, with the Christian consensus gone, the courts or some other part of government arbitrarily make the law. In the concept of genetic engineering, with the uniqueness of people as made in the image of God thrown away, mankind itself is in danger of being made over arbitrarily into the image of what some people think mankind ought to be. This will overwhelmingly be the case if such concepts as what has been called "sociobiology" are widely accepted.

According to these concepts, people do what they do because of the makeup of the genes, and the genes (in some mysterious way) know what is best for keeping the gene pool of the species flourishing. Regardless of what you think your reasons are for unselfishness, say the sociobiologists, in reality you are only doing what your genes know is best to keep your gene configuration alive and flourishing into the future. This happens because evolution has produced organisms that automatically follow a mathematical logic; they calculate the genetic costs or benefits of helping those who bear many of the same genes and act to preserve their own image. Thus, the reason why parents help their children live is that the genes of the parents make them act to preserve the future existence of like genetic forms.[5]

No one tells us how the genes got started doing this. The *how* is not known. And even if the *how* were demonstrated, the *why* would still be in total darkness. Yet with neither the *how* nor the *why* known, everything human is abandoned. Maternal love, friendships, law, and morals are all explained away. Those who hold the sociobiological view believe that conflict both in the family and with outsiders is the essence of life. This serves as a chilling reminder of Hitler's Germany, which was built on the social conclusions logically drawn from the Darwinian concept of the survival of the fittest.

Harvard zoologist Edward O. Wilson, who wrote *Sociobiology:*

The New Synthesis, says on page 562: "We may find that there is an overestimation of the nature of our deepest yearnings." He calls for "ethics to be removed temporarily from the hands of the philosophers and biologized."[6]

The humanistic philosophers tried to make ethics independent of biblical teaching; the present tragic result is the loss of humanness on every level. Now, Wilson argues, ethics and behavior patterns should be made independent of these humanistic philosophers and put into the realm of the purely mechanical, where ethics reflect only genes fighting for survival. This makes ethics equal no ethics.

Time said of sociobiology, "Indeed, few academic theories have spread so fast with so little hard proof." Why has it spread so fast with no hard proof? That is easy to explain: we have been prepared for it by all the humanistic materialism of past years. A constant barrage of authoritative, though unproven, statements comes from every side, and gradually people accept themselves and others as only machinelike things. If man is only a product of chance in an impersonal universe, and that is all there is, this teaching is a logical extension of that fact.[7]

To summarize: On the one hand, the idea that mankind is only a collection of the genes which make up the DNA patterns has naturally led to the concept of remaking all of humanity with the use of genetic engineering. On the other hand, it has led to the crime and cruelty that now disturb the very people whose teaching produces the crime and cruelty in the first place. Many of these people do not face the conclusion of their own teaching. With nothing higher than human opinion upon which to base judgments and with ethics equaling no ethics, the justification for seeing crime and cruelty as disturbing is destroyed. The very word *crime* and even the word *cruelty* lose meaning. There is no final reason on which to forbid anything—"If nothing is forbidden, then anything is possible."

If man is not made in the image of God, nothing then stands in the way of inhumanity. There is no good reason why mankind should be perceived as special. Human life is cheapened. We can see this in many of the major issues being debated in our society today: abortion, infanticide, euthanasia, the increase of child abuse and violence of all kinds, pornography (and its particular kinds of violence as evidenced in sadomasochism), the routine torture of political prisoners in many parts of the world, the crime explosion, and the random violence which surrounds us.

In communist countries, where materialism and humanistic thinking have been dominant for over several generations, a low view of people has been standard for years. This is apparent not only in the early legislation about abortion but also in the thousands of political prisoners who have been systematically oppressed, tortured, and killed as part of the very fabric of communism. Now, however, as humanism dominates the West, we have a low view of mankind in the West as well. Let us consider some more of the direct and indirect results that this low view of people has brought into our society in the noncommunist world.

Child Abuse

Dr. C. Henry Kempe, a pediatrician at the University of Colorado School of Medicine, first used the term *battered-child syndrome*. The term *child abuse* covers at least three separate entities: physical assault, physical neglect, and emotional abuse and neglect. In the first of these the child is a victim of an act of aggression.[8] These case histories are typical of thousands:

> *Case 1:* Police found a nine-year-old girl in a closet measuring twenty-three by fifty-two inches, where she had been locked for half of her life. She weighed only twenty pounds and stood less than three feet tall. Smeared with filth and scarred from parental beatings, this child had become irrevocably mentally damaged.

> *Case 2:* An eleven-year-old boy was brought to a San Francisco hospital suffering from severe malnutrition. He weighed forty-four pounds, had a body temperature of eight-four degrees, and was in coma. The suspicious marks on his wrists and ankles were related to his mother's and her boyfriend's immobilization of the boy for hours on end by means of handcuffs, chains and locks.

The second variety of child abuse, physical neglect, is probably many times more frequent than either the medical profession or the police can document. The third form, emotional abuse, is not only difficult to define but more difficult to detect and prove— after which comes the very difficult task of rehabilitative therapy.

So far it is children who have suffered the most from dehumanization. Nothing could illustrate better the dehumanization and exploitation of children than child pornography. Why doesn't public outcry demand that films depicting child pornography be withdrawn? Because the producers know that they will not be box-office failures. Dehumanization of both adults and children is taking quantum leaps. The unthinkable rapidly becomes not only thinkable but even welcome as entertainment—and being accepted as entertainment, it becomes powerful propaganda for ongoing personal and social practice, further dehumanizing young and old alike.

To begin to grasp the enormity of the problem, consider that in 1972 there were 60,000 child-abuse incidents which were brought to official attention in the United States. Just four years later, in 1976, the number that received official attention passed the half-million mark. *Reported* cases of child abuse probably represent only about half of what really occurs.

Child abuse is the fifth most frequent cause of death among children. In *U.S. News and World Report* (May 3, 1976) it was reported that Dr. Irwin Hedlener, investigating child abuse at Jackson Memorial Hospital in Miami, said: "If child abuse were polio, the whole country would be up in arms looking for a solution."

An especially alarming form of dehumanization is the apparent increase of incest. Dr. Harry Giarretto, director of the pioneering Child Sexual Abuse Treatment Center in San Jose, California, says that incest is an epidemic in America.[9] Dr. Amanat, who heads up the Sexual Abuse Committee in Saint Louis, believes that 40,000 of the 1,000,000 victims of sexual abuse a year are victims of incest. Some say that incest is the most frequent unrecorded crime in this country and much more common than general child abuse or child neglect.[10]

We believe that the increased use of children in sex films has contributed to the sexual abuse of children. When absolute sexual standards are replaced by relativistic ones, and this is coupled with the generally low view of people that modern humanists have been teaching, society is not left with many barriers against the sexual abuse of children. After you remove the psychological and moral barriers imposed by a high and sacred view of human life, child abuse of all kinds becomes very easy, given the stresses of child rearing, especially child rearing in the antifamily climate of today.[11] The Supreme Court ruling that legalized abortion and the arbitrariness of that decision regarding who is or is not a "person" have broken down barriers. There has been a drastic rise of crimes against children since abortion-on-demand became legal in the United States. We are convinced that this increase is caused in part by the liberalization of abortion laws and the resultant drastic lowering of the value placed on human life in general and on children's lives in particular.[12]

The forces of humanism have scoffed at Christian morality and ethics as well as at the Christian view of man. These theories of so-called liberation from the biblical absolutes are bearing their fruit. But humanists, far from reexamining the basis of their position now that the situation is souring, stubbornly propose (on the same old base) remedial action to the problems that humanist philosophy itself has created. This action is even more dehumanizing in its results, as we shall see later in this book.

Abortion

Of all the subjects relating to the erosion of the sanctity of human life, abortion is the keystone. It is the first and crucial issue that has been overwhelming in changing attitudes toward the value of life in general. The Supreme Court of the United States on January 22, 1973, in deciding *Roe* v. *Wade* and *Doe* v. *Bolton* declared that a new personal right or liberty existed in the Constitution—the right of a woman to procure an abortion at any time. The right of privacy was given a completely new interpretation.[13]

The Supreme Court went far beyond its own judicial function and invalidated the regulation of abortion in every state in the union. Professor John T. Noonan, Jr., professor of law at the University of California (Berkeley) said:

> Some of the legislation affected was old, going back to the mid-19th century, some was recent, reflecting the wisdom of the American Law Institute or containing explicit statements of intent to protect the fetus. Some of the legislation had been confirmed by recent popular referenda, as in Michigan and North Dakota; some of the legislation was in the process of repeal, as in New York. Old or new, compromise or complete protection from conception, passed by 19th-century males or confirmed by popular vote of both sexes, maintained by apathy or reaffirmed in vigorous democratic battle, none of the existing legislation on abortion conformed to the Court's criteria. By this basic fact alone, *Roe* v. *Wade* and *Doe* v. *Bolton* may stand as the most radical decisions ever issued by the Supreme Court.[14]

The decision of the Court went far beyond the expectation of the wildest dreams of the proabortion elite in the United States. Noonan summarized the situation this way: "By virtue of its opinions, human life has less protection in the United States today than at any time since the inception of the country. By virtue of its opinions, human life has less protection in the United States than in any country of the Western world."[15]

Archibald Cox of Watergate-prosecution fame said in his book *The Role of the Supreme Court in American Government:* "The decisions plainly . . . sweep away established law supported by the moral themes dominant in American life for more than a century in favor of what the Court takes to be the wiser view of a question under active public debate. . . . My criticism of [the decision] is that the Court failed to establish the legitimacy of decision . . . to lift the ruling above the level of political judgment."[16]

In 1977 what eventually became known as the Hyde Amendment, designed to ban the use of taxpayers' money to pay for abortion-on-demand, was repeatedly blocked by congressional technicalities. The debate on the Hyde Amendment was begun in June 1976, lasted until October, and then was passed in both houses, only to be halted by a single Brooklyn federal judge named John F. Dooling who decided that the Hyde Amendment was unconstitutional. In effect, the Supreme Court, by refusing to reverse Dooling, "gave a district court judge the power to frustrate the clearly expressed congressional will in a matter of appropriating tax funds [which] turns the doctrine of separation of powers on its head" (Congressman Hyde's words).

The Court had the opportunity to pull back from its position in a series of decisions in the summer of 1976, but instead confirmed its position and declared that a physician need not provide the same care for a living product of an abortion that would be required for a living baby delivered in a situation when the intent was to have a baby.[17]

The schizophrenic nature of our society became further evident as it became common practice for pediatricians to provide the maximum of resuscitative and supportive care in newborn intensive-care nurseries where premature infants were under their care—while obstetricians in the same medical centers were routinely destroying enormous numbers of unborn babies who were normal and frequently of larger size. Minors who could not legally purchase liquor and cigarettes could have an abortion-on-demand and without parental consent or knowledge.[18]

In our day, quite rightly, there has been great protest because society in the past viewed the black slave as a nonperson. Now, by an arbitrary absolute brought into the humanist flow, the law in similar fashion declares millions of unborn babies of every color of skin to be nonpersons. Abortion-on-demand is the law of the land, and with the erosion of society's belief in the sanctity of human life there has followed the killing of more than 1.6 million unborn babies a year. We should say here that those who favor abortion argue that child abuse will decrease if abortion is practiced. It is supposed to be kinder to the unborn child to abort it than to allow it to be born and possibly suffer mistreatment. Those who fought for liberalized abortion policies have had their way, and since 1970 it is conservatively estimated in the United States that there are probably over ten million fewer children who would now be between the ages of one and seven. Since these ten million were "unwanted" and supposedly would have been prime targets for child abuse, it would seem reasonable to look for a sharp drop in child abuse in this same period. But in fact, since the legalization of abortion-on-demand, child abuse has grown remarkably, and it is not due to just more efficient reporting.

This is because nationwide abortion-on-demand has what might be called an "educational impact." The West German Federal Constitutional Court (West Germany's Supreme Court) in its February 1975 decision banning abortion-on-demand during the first twelve weeks of pregnancy stated this: "We cannot ignore the educational impact of abortion on the respect for life." The German court reasoned that if abortion were made legal for any and every reason during the first trimester, it would prove difficult to persuade people that second- and third-trimester fetuses deserve protection simply because they are a few weeks older. The court apparently feared that what would happen to older fetuses could also happen to children after birth.[19] As Harold O. J. Brown observes, parents, perhaps unconsciously, could reason, "I didn't have to have him. I could have killed him before he was born. So if I want to knock him around now that he is born, isn't that my right?"[20]

Is it not logical, after all, that if one can legally kill a child a few months before birth, one should not feel too bad about roughing him up a little bit (without killing him) after he is born? Parents who are apprehended for child abuse must feel that the system is somewhat unfair in that they can be arrested for beating their child, whereas people who kill their infant before birth (at an "earlier age") go scot-free—in fact, have society's approval.

There is further evidence that our society is schizophrenic on these matters. Consider our concern to provide special facilities for the handicapped in public places: restrooms that can be used by someone in a wheelchair, ramps instead of steps going into public buildings, lifts on public conveyances to get a handicapped individual onto a bus or train. Yet, while having proven that we do have compassion for the handicapped as well as the resources to care for them, at the same time we have a growing tendency to destroy the newborn baby who might have been one of those handicapped individuals.

A much more serious example of this schizophrenic mentality is that we will transport a newborn baby, who is premature and has a congenital defect incompatible with life, to a hospital a considerable distance away—so that a sophisticated team of doctors and nurses can correct that defect and plan for the rehabilitation of the youngster. Meanwhile, in a number of other hospitals within gunshot distance of that center, other medical personnel are destroying perfectly normal infants in the womb.

The Growth of Human Life

Our reasons against abortion are logical as well as moral. It is impossible for anyone to say when a developing fetus becomes viable, that is, has the ability to exist on its own. Smaller and smaller premature infants are being saved each year! There was a day when a 1000-gram preemie had no chance; now 50 percent of preemies under 1000 grams are being saved. Theoretically, there once was a point beyond which technology could not be expected to go in salvaging premature infants—but with further technological advances, who knows what the limits may be! The eventual possibilities are staggering.

The logical approach is to go back to the sperm and the egg. A sperm has twenty-three chromosomes; even though it is alive and can fertilize an egg, it can never make another sperm. An egg also has twenty-three chromosomes, and it can never make another egg. Thus, we have sperm that cannot reproduce and eggs that cannot reproduce unless they get together. Once the union of a sperm and an egg occurs and the twenty-three chromosomes of each are brought together into one cell that has forty-six chromosomes, that one cell has all the DNA (the whole genetic code) that will, if not interrupted, make a human being.[21]

Our question to a proabortion doctor who would not kill a *newborn* baby is this: "Would you then kill this infant a minute before he was born, or a minute before that, or a minute before that, or a minute before that?" At what point in time can one consider life to be worthless and the next minute precious and worth saving?

Having already mentioned the union of sperm and egg to give forty-six chromosomes, let us briefly review the development of a baby. At twenty-one days, the first irregular beats occur in the developing heart, long before the mother is sure she is pregnant. Forty-five days after conception, electroencephalographic waves can be picked up from the baby's developing brain.

By the ninth and tenth weeks, the thyroid and the adrenal glands are functioning. The baby can squint, swallow, and move his tongue. The sex hormones are already present. By twelve or thirteen weeks, he has fingernails; he sucks his thumb and will recoil from pain. His fingerprints, on the hands which have already formed, will never change throughout his lifetime except for size. Legally, it is understood that an individual's fingerprints distinguish him as a separate identity and are the most difficult characteristic to falsify.

In the fourth month the growing baby is eight to ten inches long. The fifth month is a time of lengthening and strengthening. Skin, hair, and nails grow. Sweat glands come into being; oil glands excrete. This is the month in which the mother feels the infant's movements.

In the sixth month the developing baby responds to light and sound. He can sleep and awaken. He gets hiccups and can hear the beat of his mother's heart. Survival outside the womb is now possible. In the seventh month the nervous system becomes much more complex. The infant is about sixteen inches long and weighs about three pounds. The eighth and ninth months see a fattening of the baby.

We do not know how anyone who has seen the remarkable films of the intrauterine development of the human embryo can still maintain that the product of an abortion consists of just some membranes or a part of the woman's body over which she has complete control—or indeed anything other than a human life within the confines of a tiny body. At the very least we must admit that an embryo is not simply an extension of another person's body; it is something separate and uniquely irreplaceable. Another good reason we should not view the unborn baby as an extension of the woman's body is that it did not originate only from the woman. The baby would not exist without the man's seed.

We are convinced that the reason the Supreme Court decision for abortion-on-demand never came to grips with the issue of the viability of the human fetus is that its viability (that is, ability to live outside the womb on its own) is really not the important point.

Viable or not, the single-celled fertilized egg will develop into a human being unless some force destroys its life. We should add that biologists take the uniform position that life begins at conception; there is no logical reason why the proabortionist should try to arrive at a different definition when he is talking about people, the highest form of all biological creatures. After conception, no additional factor is necessary at a later time. All that makes up the adult is present as the ovum and the sperm are united—the whole genetic code is present.

Abortion Techniques
There are three commonly used techniques for abortion. The technique used most often to end early pregnancies is called the D & C or *dilation and curettage*. In this procedure, usually carried out before the twelfth or thirteenth week of pregnancy, the uterus is approached through the vagina. The cervix is stretched to permit the insertion of a curette, a tiny hoelike instrument. The surgeon then scrapes the wall of the uterus, cutting the baby's body to pieces and scraping the placenta from its attachments on the uterine wall. Bleeding is considerable.

An alternate method which is used during the same period of pregnancy is called *suction abortion*. The principle is the same as in the D & C. A powerful suction tube is inserted through the dilated cervix into the uterus. This tears apart the body of the developing baby and the placenta, sucking the pieces into a jar. The smaller parts of the body are recognizable as arms, legs, head, and so on. More than two-thirds of all abortions performed in the United States and Canada apparently are done by this method.

Later in pregnancy, when the D & C or suction abortion might produce too much bleeding in the expectant mother, doctors employ the second most common abortion technique, called the *saline abortion,* or "salting out." This method is usually carried out after sixteen weeks of pregnancy, when enough amniotic fluid has accumulated in the sac around the baby. A long needle is inserted through the mother's abdomen directly into the sac, and a solution of concentrated salt is injected into the amniotic fluid. The salt solution is absorbed both through the lungs and the gastrointestinal tract, producing changes in the osmotic pressure. The outer layer of skin is burned off by the high concentration of salt. It takes about an hour to kill the baby by this slow method. The mother usually goes into labor about a day later and delivers a dead, shriveled baby.

If abortion is decided on too late to be accomplished by either a D & C, suction, or saline procedure, physicians resort to a final technique called *hysterotomy*. A hysterotomy is exactly the same as a Cesarean section with one difference—in a Cesarean section the operation is usually performed to save the life of the baby, whereas a hysterotomy is performed to kill the baby. These babies look very much like other babies except that they are small and weigh, for example, about two pounds at the end of a twenty-four-week pregnancy. They are truly alive, but they are allowed to die through neglect or sometimes killed by a direct act.

Hysterotomy gives the fetus the best chance for survival, but at a very high price in morbidity for the mother—fifteen times greater than that of saline infusion, the more commonly used alternative. In 1977 a Boston jury found Dr. Kenneth Edelin guilty of manslaughter for killing the product of this type of abortion.[22]

That children are often born alive after abortions is fact and not a new phenomenon. A brief in one case before the Supreme Court (*Markle* v. *Abele*) contained a table listing twenty-seven live births after abortions.[23] That was in 1972. In the first year of liberalized abortion laws in New York State, before the Supreme Court decision regarding abortion-on-demand, some of those "products of abortions" were eventually adopted.

Nothing is more embarrassing to an abortionist than to deliver a live baby. To show that this is so, the following is a quote from a publication of the International Correspondence Society of Obstetrics and Gynecologists (November 1974):

> At the time of delivery it has been our policy to wrap the fetus in a towel. The fetus is then moved to another room while our attention is turned to the care of the gravida [the former mother-to-be]. She is examined to determine whether placenta expulsion has occurred and the extent of vaginal bleeding. Once we are sure her condition is stable, the fetus is evaluated. Almost invariably all signs of life have ceased.

What a nice little piece of "how to" instruction!

It was once thought that live births after abortions would be possible only after hysterotomies. Now it is obvious that babies are born alive after saline abortions as well. Dr. William G. Waddill, Jr., an obstetrician in California, was indicted and tried in January 1977 for allegedly strangling to death a baby born alive following a saline abortion.

An interminable trial got out of hand when the issue departed from whether or not Waddill had indeed attempted to strangle a living infant. The trial resulted in a hung jury when the judge introduced for deliberation new material concerning a California definition of death, which really had little bearing on this subject. The former mother-to-be of the allegedly strangled infant filed suit for $17,000,000 on grounds that she was not adequately informed of the possible outcome of the abortion and that she had suffered long-lasting physical and emotional pain as a result of the doctor's actions.[24]

If live babies as a result of saline abortions and hysterotomies cause problems for the abortionist, they are minor compared to the problems that have been introduced by the prostaglandin method of abortion. The use of prostaglandin has multiplied the number of embarrassing situations manifold. Prostaglandin is a hormone which has practically no other use except to induce abortions. Upjohn manufactures it in the United States, and in September 1977 the Food and Drug Administration approved it for use in hospitals. It is advertised in the pharmacy reports as "Prostin E. Upjohn abortion inducer." This warning was carried in the September 12, 1977, issue of *Weekly Pharmacy Reports,* pointing out the approved Prostin labeling notes that suppository form, unlike saline injection form, "does not appear to directly effect the integrity of the feto-placental unit and therefore, there exists a possibility that a live-born fetus may occur, particularly as gestational age approaches the end of the second trimester." So likely is a live birth after a prostaglandin abortion that a medical representative of Upjohn advises using Prostin E. "only in hospitals with certain intensive care facilities."[25]

Although technically the product of a legal abortion, each fetus expelled alive because of prostaglandin lives for several hours, later has to be pronounced dead by a physician, must receive both a birth and death certificate, and is sent to a funeral director for burial or cremation.

Live Births After Abortions

Physicians have been reluctant to reveal the number of second-trimester abortions (during the second three-month period of pregnancy) that result in live births. Of 607 such abortions done at Mount Sinai Hospital in Hartford, Connecticut, forty-five resulted in live births, including one set of twins. All of these forty-five babies were taken to the neonatal nursery for active resuscitation. Physicians there decided how long to consider resuscitation, according to the infant's weight, neurological maturity, and general condition. None of the babies survived more than thirteen hours, despite attempts to save them. These infants were born following an intra-amniotic injection of prostaglandin, and we would expect that the suppository form would produce more, not fewer, of these embarrassing situations for abortionists.

It could be said in passing that there were other complications in addition to the live births in the second-trimester abortions at Mount Sinai. Excessive blood loss occurred in 19.4 percent of the women; 41 percent had incomplete abortions, in which case the placenta had to be removed manually. The Mount Sinai series was reported by Dr. Wing K. Lee at an Atlanta meeting in 1977.[26]

Other presentations at that same clinical congress reported that hypertonic saline injections for mid-trimester abortions beyond twenty weeks produce a higher rate of other complications. In spite of that, at least the Nassau County Medical Center in East Meadow, New York, decided to return to that form of treatment rather than have the embarrassment of live births. Dr. Joel Robins of the Stony Brook branch of the State University of New York compared 700 prostaglandin with 170 saline abortions. He found it was not such a bad idea to switch back to saline, because the rates of complication were similar and there were seven live births with prostaglandin and none with saline.[27]

It remained for a Johns Hopkins University team to introduce an economic factor. They added hyperosmoler urea to augment the prostaglandin. The combined technique was reported to have a lower failure rate and a lower cost. Since the urea dilates the cervix, the Hopkins group found that it is easier to remove fetal parts than with a D & C and that the process carries a lower coagulation risk than saline.[28]

We would like to assume the role of prophet and say that since the FDA has approved Prostin E. by Upjohn as an abortion inducer, we think they will before long give Upjohn the approval to market a vaginal tampon with prostaglandin on its tip, which will be advertised as an inducer of menstruation. This would then bring to its logical conclusion Justice Blackmun's statement that the right of privacy covers his decision about abortion-on-demand. With such a menses inducer, any woman could use a vaginal tampon containing Prostin E. once a month and never know whether she was having a normal menstrual period or an abortion. Thus, abortion could become a totally private affair. The only good we can see coming out of that terrible situation is that at least it would eliminate the abortionist.

Inasmuch as the live product (i.e., a living baby, although not necessarily able to support itself outside the womb) of a prostaglandin abortion lives for several hours after the abortion—and so must be pronounced dead by a physician, receives both birth and death certificates, and needs management by a funeral director for burial or cremation—it is clear that there can be considerable consternation and emotional upset on the part of the hospital staff, particularly the nurses and paramedical attendants at the time of "delivery."

In 1977 the nurses and medical staff at Hollywood's Memorial Hospital (Florida) rebelled after several live fetuses were born during second-trimester abortions. Hospital Administrator Sal Mudano commented, "We've had preemies that have lived that were less developed than some of these abortions were. Our personnel are not in favor of working in that kind of situation, and the law says we can't force people to participate against their personal or religious beliefs." And he added, "It's not that we're preaching, and we don't have a bunch of religious fanatics on our staff. But our nurses are geared to saving lives and this is just the opposite."[29]

According to the *Fort Lauderdale News,* officials at Broward General Hospital in Fort Lauderdale feel as if they are forced to walk a tightrope between providing a legally sanctioned service demanded by the public and living up to their duty to save lives. "The law is not really clear on whether a publicly supported hospital can limit the type of abortions it offers," said a hospital spokesman.

The nursing supervisor at Hollywood Memorial, Joann Kopacka, said, "The use of prostaglandin was totally unacceptable. Philosophically, it was a very difficult thing to handle for the nurses. The live fetus is not an 'it,' or a thing, it is a life."

Mudano said the antiabortion feeling among the staff at Memorial is so strong that doctors generally take their second-trimester abortion cases elsewhere. "We're down to six or eight saline solution abortions a month, which is significantly less than when we started doing them," Mudano said. "That's the result of our philosophy of discouraging them."

Mrs. Jean Moore, supervisor of the obstetrical nurses at Broward General for seventeen years, said the nurses at the hospital have not reacted as emotionally as the nurses at Hollywood. "We can't see that they are reacting any differently when a live fetus is born," Mrs. Moore said. "The nurses who work in this area know what to expect. They feel that they are there to assist the physician. We really don't have any problems among the nurses."

A hospital spokesman said the lack of problems with the nurses at Broward General was due to good scheduling by Mrs. Moore. "She is careful not to put anyone with strong feelings about abortions in that area," he said. "We try to arrange the schedules so that those who prefer not to be involved are not, unless it is absolutely necessary."

A doctor said he has never seen any adverse reactions on the part of the Broward General staff when a live fetus is born. "When you have a ten-ounce fetus with spontaneous respiration or movement, it is more upsetting to the lay public than to anybody else. The hospital procedure is almost mechanical at this point. It kind of works very smoothly."[30]

As another example, a publication of Nurses Concerned for Life, Inc., considered these facts, reported in the *Pittsburgh Press* on November 1, 1974:

A 26-year-old woman requested an abortion of her 5-month fetus, claiming that she had been raped. The woman was first turned down by Magee Woman's Hospital because it was thought the pregnancy was too far advanced. The staff physician estimated the gestational age to be about 25 weeks. It was later established that she had not been raped.

The abortion was then performed by Dr. Leonard Laufe of West Penn Hospital in Pittsburgh, Pa., who decided to use the prostaglandin method. Prostaglandin is an abortifacient drug whose primary effect is stimulation of the uterine contractions. Its use frequently leads to a live birth. Nurse Monica Bright testified that the child gasped for breath for at least 15 minutes following the abortion and no attempts were made to help the child in any way. Ms. Bright is a circulating nurse in Labor and Delivery. She further testified that she observed a pulse in the upper chest, left neck area. Ms. Shirley Foust, R.N., testified she had seen the baby move and that one of the foreign residents, who was observing, baptized the child. The Head Nurse, Carol Totton, testified that the baby was gasping and a pulse was visible. Both the nurse anaesthetist and Ms. Totton refused to administer a lethal dose of morphine to the baby despite the fact that "someone in the room had ordered it."

The nurse anaesthetist, Nancy Gaskey, testified that the abortion was performed in a room where there were no resuscitative measures available if the child was born alive.

The entire procedure was filmed for educational purposes and the film showed the baby moving. Dr. Jules Rivkind, Chairman, Department of OB and Gyn, at Mercy Hospital, testified that this was indeed "a live birth."

The original birth records indicate the baby girl weighed 3 lbs. 1 ounce and listed the length as 45 centimeters. Dr. Laufe later changed the hospital records to read as follows: weight 2 lbs. 9 oz., length 29 centimeters. Lois Cleary, a staff nurse, witnessed this change, and testified that in the 3,000 to 4,000 births she had assisted with there had never been such changes made on original records to her knowledge. This change was also verified by an OB technician who was present. Estimated gestational age 29 to 32 weeks.

John Kenny, a young medical student, testified that he had been threatened by Dr. Laufe's attorney if he testified in court against Dr. Laufe. The young man was told that he would be unable to get an internship in any hospital in Pennsylvania if he testified. He was also told he would be unable to get a license to practice medicine.

Editor's note [You Be the Judge]—Dr. Laufe was acquitted of the charges because he claimed the baby's brain was dead due to damage caused when he clamped the umbilical arteries in utero.[31]

Embryos "created" in the biologists' laboratories raise special questions because they have the potential for growth and development if planted in the womb. The disposal of these live embryos is a cause for ethical and moral concern. Dr. Leon Kass, a University of Chicago biologist, wonders:

> Who decides what are the grounds for discard? What if there is another recipient available who wishes to have the otherwise unwanted embryo? Whose embryos are they? The woman's? The couple's? The geneticist's? The obstetrician's? The Ford Foundation's? Shall we say that discarding laboratory grown embryos is a matter solely between a doctor and his plumber? . . . We have paid some high prices for the technological conquest of nature, but none so high

as the intellectual and spiritual costs of seeing nature as mere material for our manipulation, exploitation and transformation. With the powers for biological engineering now gathering, there will be splendid new opportunities for a similar degradation of our view of man. Indeed, we are already witnessing the erosion of our idea of man as something splendid or divine, as a creature with freedom and dignity. And clearly, if we come to see ourselves as meat, then meat we shall become.[32]

There are many unpleasant spin-offs from the basic ugliness of the abortion scene. One is that fewer babies are available for adoption. More childless couples remain childless. This seems especially ironic when one considers that many abortions are being performed very late in term and that a prospective mother could, with little more physical trauma, wait to deliver a normal child at full term and give it up for adoption. That this is not done more often raises the question as to whether in certain cases the mother-to-be does not have an instinctive attachment to the unborn child. That she anticipates the sorrow the separation will bring—and would rather kill the child than lose it—testifies to the fact that the mother knows subconsciously that she has in her womb something more than the mere glob of protoplasm the abortionist would have her believe she is carrying.

Obviously, many more babies are unwanted early in pregnancy than is the case later in pregnancy or after birth. It is the ready availability of abortion-on-demand, when a pregnant woman first has that natural question about how well she can handle a pregnancy, that leads to the tremendous number of abortions. This can be put in personal terms by asking people, "If abortion-on-demand had been available to your mother when she first heard she was pregnant with you, would you be here today?"

Recently several local and state abortion regulations have stipulated that some time must elapse between the woman's decision to abort and the actual procedure. The Akron ordinance passed in March 1978 is the prototype for such legislation. Such legislation does not ban abortion (a ban that would be unconstitutional at the present time), but it does impose some controls. The Akron regulation requires that parents of pregnant girls under eighteen be notified before an abortion is performed. The ordinance also requires that a woman receive counseling by a physician about the results of abortion and that at least twenty-four hours must pass before the abortion can be performed. This provision of course gives a woman more time to think through a hasty decision, so that there will be less chance that she will regret it later.[33]

Current sexual mores, sexually permissive life-styles, and the breakdown of the family demand abortion. At the same time the availability of abortion contributes to a change in our sexual mores, our permissive life-styles, and general family break-down—truly a vicious cycle. The changes in the technical aspects of medicine are almost staggering. It is said that about 90 percent of the current body of medical knowledge has been learned in the last twenty-five years. We can only regret that ethical views of the medical profession, and of society in general, have not kept pace with the technological advances.

That over a million unborn children die each year at the hands of abortionists is sufficient reason for the ardor of those who oppose abortion. When one sees the potential of handicapped youngsters realized through surgery, sees the blessing they are to their families, sees how loved and loving they are themselves, it makes it impossible for some to stand by while millions of normal babies are being killed before birth and discriminated against on so large a scale. As individuals who have marveled at the unique personalities of even the tiniest infants, something basically human in us is revolted by the thought of wanton slaughter of the unborn.

Three Final Issues
First, why is it that so few abortion counselors are fair to the "whole person" of the pregnant woman? "Why didn't anyone tell me?" is a fair question from a girl suffering the aftereffects of a recommended abortion.[34] "Why didn't anyone tell me I would feel like a mother with empty arms?" "Why didn't anyone tell me I risked spoiling the possibility of having a normal pregnancy, because of the damage that might be done to my body by the abortion?" These are not just theoretical questions put forth in an abstract academic debate. Abortion counselors rarely talk about physical dangers, emotional results, and psychological conse-quences. They seldom tell the woman what is going to happen or what may be involved.[35]

We need to think seriously about the aborted human beings who have been deprived of a chance to live, but we also need to consider with sympathy and compassion the women being turned into "aborted mothers"—bereft mothers—bitter in some cases, hard in some cases, exceedingly sorrowful in other cases. It is unfair not to make the options clear. To tell a pregnant woman that a few hours or a day in the hospital or clinic will rid her of all her problems and will send her out the door a free person is to forget the humanness of women who are now mothers. With many of the women who have had abortions, their "motherliness" is very much present even though the child is gone.

Abortion does not end all the problems; often it just exchanges one set for another. Whether or not one believes in the reality of guilt is *not* the question at this point. One of the facts of being a human being is that in spite of the abnormality of human beings and the cruelty of their actions, there still exist the hopes and fears, the longings and aspirations, that can be bundled together in the word *motherliness*. To stamp out these feelings is to insure that many women will turn into the kind of hard people they may not want to be. For others, it is a bewildering nightmare to be overwhelmed with longings for the baby to be back in them and to be able to complete that which had begun. To assume that all women will want to abort—and to give flat advice without explaining the very real problems some aborted mothers have—is cruelty in the wrappings of blasé and glib kindness.

Second, abortion is not a "Roman Catholic issue." This must be emphasized. Those who favor abortion often try to minimize the arguments of those who oppose it by conveying the idea that only the Roman Catholic Church is against abortion. We must indeed be glad for the Roman Catholics who have spoken out, but we must not allow the position to be minimized as though it is a "religious" issue. It is not a religious issue.

This line of attack has been carried so far that some lawyers want to rule out the entrance of Congress and the courts into the discussion at all, on the basis that it is only a Roman Catholic issue and therefore a violation of the separation of church and state. The issue, however, is not "divided along religious lines," and it has nothing to do with the separation of church and state.[36]

The issue of the humanness of the unborn child is one raised by many people across a vast spectrum of religious backgrounds, and, happily, also by thousands who have no religion at all. A picture in the *International Herald Tribune* of January 25, 1978, showed a Washington protest march on the fifth anniversary of the Supreme Court decision that restricted the rights of states to regulate and thereby curtail the spread of abortion. The most outstanding sign being carried read: IF MY MOM DIDN'T CARE—I MIGHT NOT BE HERE—THANKS, MOM! The young girl carrying that sign did not have to be religious to paint and carry it; all she needed was to be glad she was not aborted. And the right of that girl to express her views on life and death to those who represent her in the democratic process and to be heard in the courts depends only on her being a citizen of the United States. Abortion is not a religious issue. It is a human issue!

Nor is abortion a feminist issue, any more than slavery was only a slave owners' issue. Abortion has been tacked onto the feminist issue, with the feminist issue being used to carry abortion. But there is no intrinsic relationship between them. The fate of the unborn is a question of the fate of the human race. We are one human family. If the rights of one part of that family are denied, it is of concern to each of us. What is at stake is no less than the essence of what freedom and rights are all about.[37]

Third, when the United States Supreme Court made its ruling about abortion on January 22, 1973, Mr. Justice Blackmun delivered the opinion of the Court. The first section in his opinion was titled "Ancient Attitudes." In it he referred back to pre-Christian law. He said, "Greek and Roman law afforded little protection to the unborn. If abortion was prosecuted in some places, it seems to have been based on a concept of a violation of the father's right to his offspring. Ancient religion did not bar abortion." Thus, as his first point, Mr. Justice Blackmun based his opinion on the practice of pre-Christian Greek and Roman law. Most people who read this did not realize the logical result concerning babies after their birth. Roman law permitted not only abortion but also infanticide. As we think this over, we ask ourselves, "Now that this door is open, how long will it be before infanticide is socially accepted and perhaps legalized?"

CHAPTER TWO

The Slaughter of the Innocents

Infanticide is not yet legalized, but the law is strangely silent about what amounts to public confessions in reputable scientific journals by medical doctors who admit that they are indeed practicing it. Infanticide is the killing of a born child—whether that killing is accomplished by a direct act on the part of someone, or whether ordinary care vital to the child's survival, such as feeding, is refused. It makes little difference whether infanticide is direct or indirect. Either way a child is killed.

The first effort we know of in this country to educate the medical profession in the art of infanticide was a documentary motion picture titled *Who Shall Survive?* Johns Hopkins Hospital and Medical School produced it in 1972. It shows a newborn infant with Down's syndrome (frequently called mongolism) who was permitted to die by "inattention." We suspect that "starving to death" would be a more accurate way of saying this.

People who have never had the experience of working with children who are being rehabilitated into our society after the correction of a congenital defect often say that infants with such defects should be allowed to die or even "encouraged" to die, because their lives can obviously be nothing but unhappy and miserable. Yet it is constantly to be observed that disability and unhappiness do not necessarily go together. Some of the most unhappy children have all of their physical and mental faculties, while some of the happiest youngsters have borne burdens which most of us would find very difficult to endure.

The obligation in such circumstances is to find alternatives for the problems such children and their parents face. Morally and logically, we do not consider infanticide an acceptable alternative. With today's technology and creativity, we are merely at the beginning of what we can do to help such youngsters with formal educational and leisure-time activities.

Who knows what constitutes "happiness" for another person? And what about the rewards and satisfactions that come to those who succeed in rehabilitating other-than-perfect children? Stronger character, compassion, deeper understanding of another's burden, creativity, and deeper family bonds—all these can and do result from the so-called social burden of raising a child with a congenital defect.

The Medical Profession Views Infanticide

Infanticide is being practiced right now in this country, and the saddest thing about it is that it is being carried on by the very segment of the medical profession which has always stood in the role of advocate for the lives of children. The fully developed view of the medical profession in the West grew out of the Christian consensus, and, as we have seen, stands in sharp contrast to old Roman customs. The traditional view of the medical profession has been well stated by J. Engelburt Dunphy, Robert D. Zachary, and Peter Paul Rickham. Dunphy is one of the great teachers of American surgery in this generation. Zachary is the senior pediatric surgical consultant at Children's Hospital of Sheffield, England. He has been in the forefront of developing operations for the correction of spina bifida and its complications: orthopedic defects and hydrocephalus (water on the brain). Rickham is professor of pediatric surgery at the University of Zurich and has been a pioneer in developing surgery and intensive care for the newborn.

Dunphy said in the annual oration before the Massachusetts Medical Society in 1976:

> We cannot destroy life. We cannot regard the hydrocephalic child as
> a nonperson and accept the responsibility for disposing of it like a sick
> animal. If there are those in society who think this step would be

good, let them work for a totalitarian form of government where, beginning with the infirm and incompetent and ending with the intellectually dissident, nonpersons are disposed of day and night by those in power.

History shows clearly the frighteningly short steps from "the living will" to "death control" to "thought control" and finally to the systematic elimination of all but those selected for slavery or to make up the master race. We physicians must take care that support of an innocent but quite unnecessary "living will" does not pave the way for us to be the executioners while the decisions for death are made by a panel of "objective experts" or by big brother himself. The year of 1984 is not far away!

Robert D. Zachary, on July 9, 1976, in the Forshall Lecture given before the British Association of Pediatric Surgeons in Sheffield, England, said:

> I believe that our patients, no matter how young or small they are, should receive the same consideration and expert help that would be considered normal in an adult. Just because he is small, just because he cannot speak for himself, this is no excuse to regard him as expendable, any more than we would do so on account of race or creed or color or poverty. Nor do I think we ought to be swayed by an argument that the parents have less to lose because he is small and newborn, and has not yet established a close relationship with them, or indeed because the infant himself does not know what he is losing, by missing out on life.

Zachary concluded his lecture with these comments:

> There are some ways in which modern society cares greatly about those who are less well off: the poor, the sick, and the handicapped, but it seems to me that newborn babies are often given less than justice. Our primary concern must be the well-being of the patient— as far as it is in our power to achieve it. In his battle at the beginning of life, it could well be that his main defense will be in the hands of pediatric and neonatal surgeons.[38]

At the hundredth anniversary of Children's Hospital in Sheffield, England, in an address titled "The Swing of the Pendulum," Professor Rickham said:

> How many normal newborn infants will live happily ever after, especially in our present time? It may be argued that by not selecting, we artificially increase the number of people with an unhappy future, but can we be sure of this in any given case? After all, doctors deal with single, individual patients and not with statistical possibilities. It

has also been pointed out that even a child with a grave physical and mental handicap can experience emotions such as happiness, fright, gratitude and love and that it may be therefore, in fact, a rewarding task to look after him. It has been further argued that, strictly speaking, selection implies a limitation of resources, because with an optimum of resources and care a great deal can be done for these children and their families. In underdeveloped countries these resources do not exist, but in developed countries, where such enormous sums are spent by governments on purposes which are of very doubtful benefit to humanity at large, the distribution of resources is a debatable subject. Finally, it can be argued that if selection is practiced, it may not be necessarily the fittest on whom the greatest effort should be expended.

The late Lord Cohen of Birkenhead, a man whose name is associated with the beginnings of the National Health Service in Great Britain, had this to say about the possibility of killing British children who are mentally defective or epileptic: "No doctor could subscribe to this view . . . who has seen the love and devotion which brings out all that is best in men when lavished on such a child."

In 1975 the Sonoma Conference (in California) on Ethical Issues in Neonatal Intensive Care produced a 193-page report titled "Ethics of Newborn Intensive Care." At the conference, seventeen members of a panel of twenty answered yes to this question: "Would it be right to directly intervene to kill a self-sustaining infant?" (A self-sustaining infant is a child who can live without technical assistance of any kind. That means he can survive with no help other than normal feeding.) One of the marks of our time is that many of the nonphysicians on the panel, including bioethicists, lawyers, a nurse, a social worker, a sociologist, an anthropologist, and a philosopher, could see no difference at all between not putting a child on a machine and not giving it food. Letting a dying child die and actually killing a living child by starvation were all the same to them. The physicians on the panel said they themselves would hesitate to kill such an infant directly, but would not prevent someone else from doing so. This is total relativism. Values are a purely subjective matter and could change with any circumstance.

A widely read monthly newspaper for pediatricians called *Pediatric News* posed questions to three physicians concerning the 1975 Sonoma Conference report. *Pediatric News* devoted a large portion of its April 1977 issue to the answers, which are most significant in a discussion of the implications of this problem—the wrong answers to which can shape the foundations of the futures for us all.

One of the physicians quizzed was Dr. George M. Ryan, Jr., of Boston Hospital for Women. He said:

> The most difficult question is obviously whether it would ever be right to intervene directly to kill a self-sustaining infant. It is relatively easy to conceive of ceasing to provide unnatural prolongation of meaningless life by technology, but to actively kill an infant that is living without this support is to me repugnant. I think this action is so in conflict with the concept of the physician as a "healer" that such a decision should not be thrust upon the medical profession. Clearly the physician can testify as to the physical and medical status of the patient and can even predict some of the elements of the general human potential of the individual, but beyond this point, the physician has no special talent or training not available to the rest of society that might provide him with the capability of making infallible decisions. I am not very sanguine about the wisdom of any one group in making such decisions.

We certainly agree with Dr. Ryan on how repugnant this situation is. We agree, too, that physicians have no corner on the market in making infallible decisions, even though they certainly have some knowledge that is not available to the average consumer of health care. The point is that no one should be making decisions to kill self-sustaining infants.

Another of the three physicians was asked his opinion about the Sonoma Conference findings. Dr. R. T. F. Schmidt of Cincinnati, at that time president-elect of the American College of Obstetrics and Gynecologists, answered from the point of view of traditional moral and ethical standards. He said, "The fact that seventeen of twenty expert panelists believe that some severely defective infants should be killed under certain conditions is deeply disturbing. This position is not only deeply disturbing to our traditional concept of the inherent value of human life but is potentially shattering to the foundations of Western civilization."

Dr. Schmidt was careful to point out that much of the Sonoma Conference represented sound deliberation, but he felt that the issue of infanticide is of such far-reaching importance that it deserves to be singled out. He concluded his remarks by saying:

> Finally, the issue was clouded by questions raised as to what state of

perfection or imperfection qualifies a human being as a person. The Supreme Court decision of 1973 has already severely limited this qualification. Under current law, the existence of every future member of our society may be terminated [within the uterus] according to the value judgment of one or, at the most, two private individuals. To extend this contingency of private value judgment to the newborn infant in either ethical standard or in law would be another ominous step backward.

The Decision to Kill

Although the following headline is unfair to Dr. Victor Vaughn, an ethical and reputable pediatrician and educator, once chief at St. Christopher's Hospital in Philadelphia, the fact that such a headline could appear in a medical newspaper in 1977 should jolt us to the very foundation of our being: M.D.-PARENT DECISION NEEDED TO KILL INFANT. One only has to read the article to see that it is considered unwise for a parent to decide by himself to kill his child, or for a physician to decide by himself to kill the parent's child, but that their consensus makes such a decision legitimate.

Dr. John A. Robertson of the University of Wisconsin Law School and Medical School spoke what seems to us a word of wisdom to bring this discussion down to earth. He said that "one must decide for whose benefit is the decision to withhold treatment from a child with severe birth defects. Is no life better than one of low quality? The person to ask is an individual who has a disabling birth defect." Let us emphasize: *The person to ask is an individual who has a disabling birth defect.*

In preparing for the writing of this book, we did just that and something more. Four patients of one of us—born with congenital defects incompatible with life (who had been operated upon on the first day or two of life)—were assembled with four other children who had developed lethal problems in early childhood. They were not coached in any way concerning what answers they were to give to questions. They were told that we were making some documentary movies and were writing a book on the general topic of "Whatever Happened to the Human Race?" We allowed them to talk with each other for about an hour, in order to feel comfortable before being asked to participate in our plans.

The patients at the time ranged in age from eleven to thirty years. One patient had been born with a number of major congenital defects down the midline of his body, requiring twenty-seven operative procedures for correction. Another was born without an esophagus, requiring a transplantation of the colon to replace the absent organ. Still another was born with a tumor of the tongue, necessitating almost total amputation of that structure in a series of operations. The final youngster with congenital defects was born with major defects of the esophagus, the lower bowel, and the bladder.

The other four children all had tumors. One was a benign tumor of the bones of the face, which had required a number of operations for correction and still had not achieved perfection. The other three had cancers of the adrenal gland, of the parotid gland, and of the uterus.

There can be no doubt about how such young people feel about the joy of living, despite the time-consuming and usually painful medical and surgical procedures they have endured to correct birth defects or those discovered in early childhood. Here is a sampling of their comments:

> Because the start was a little abnormal, it doesn't mean you're going to finish that way. I'm a normal, functioning human being, capable of doing anything anyone else can. . . .

> At times it got very hard, but life is certainly worth living. I married a wonderful guy and I'm just so happy. . . .

> At the beginning it was a little difficult going back to school after surgery, but then things started looking up, with a little perseverance and support. I am an anesthetist and I'm happily married. Things are going great for me. . . .

> I really think that all my operations and all the things I had wrong with me were worth it, because I really enjoy life and I don't really let the things that are wrong with me bother me. . . .

> If anything, I think I've had an added quality to my life—an appreciation of life. I look forward to every single morning. . . .

> Most of the problems are what my parents went through with the surgery. I've now been teaching high school for eight years and it's a great joy. . . .

> They spend millions of dollars to send men to the moon. I think they can spend any amount necessary to save someone's life. A human life is so important because it's a gift—not something that you can give, so you really don't have the right to take it either. . . .

> I really don't consider myself handicapped. Life is just worth living. What else can I say? . . .

One of our special friends is Craig, who was a student at L'Abri in Switzerland. He is a graduate in philosophy from Cal State and is now a theological student at Covenant Seminary. He was born without a left leg and without arms below the elbows. Today, in some hospitals, Craig might have been deliberately allowed to die at birth, on the mistaken assumption that life is not worth living for the seriously handicapped person. When we asked Craig what he thought about those who say that people born with such serious birth defects should be eliminated, this, in part, was his reply:

> They don't really see that what they are talking about is murder. I know, when I was born, the first thing my dad said to my mom was that "this one needs our love more." An individual with a handicap needs our love and needs us to help him grow into the being that God has made him to be. They are advocating that we destroy these children before they're even given a chance to live and to conquer their handicaps.
>
> I'm very glad to be alive. I live a full, meaningful life. I have many friends and many things that I want to do in life. I think the secret of living with a handicap is realizing who you are—that you're a human being, somebody who is very special—looking at the things that you *can* do in spite of your handicap, and maybe even through your handicap.

Those who graduated from medical school in the first half of this century probably came out of that experience with the idea that they had been trained to "alleviate suffering and save lives." The suffering to be relieved was the *patient's* suffering and the life to be saved was the *patient's* life. This has become distorted in the semantics of the euthanasia movement in the following way. Doctors are to save lives; that is part of their profession. If the life they are trying to save, however, is producing suffering on the part of the family, doctors are to allay that suffering by disposing of their patient. So, in a strange way, it can still be said that doctors are alleviating suffering and saving lives. But the practice of infanticide for the well-being of the family is a far cry from the traditional role of the pediatrician and more lately of the pediatric surgeon.

Abortion, infanticide, and euthanasia are not only questions for women and other relatives directly involved—nor are they the prerogatives of a few people who have thought through the wider ramifications. They are life-and-death issues that concern the whole human race and should be addressed as such. Putting pressure on the public and on legislators to accept a lower view of human beings, small groups of people often argue their case by using a few extreme examples to gain sympathy for ideas and practices that later are not limited to extreme cases. These then become the common practice of the day. Abortion, for example, has moved from something once considered unusual and now in many cases is an accepted form of "birth control."

Infanticide is following the same pattern. The argument begins with people who have a so-called vegetative existence. There then follows a tendency to expand the indications and eliminate almost any child who is unwanted for some reason.

The same movement can be seen with euthanasia. The arguments now being put forward center on the "miserable" person in old age—one dying of cancer, for instance. But once the doors are open, there is no reason why the aged, weak, and infirm will not find that as they become economic burdens they will be eliminated under one pretext or another.

At first we hear much talk of compassion for the unwanted. The discussion moves on to "rights," then to "my" rights and soon to pure "economics." The discussion of life must be brought back to where it belongs—not to emotional, extreme examples, not to selfish questions of rights, not to expedience, and certainly not to economics.[39] The matter should be discussed in terms of right and wrong.

How Should We Then Live? spoke of "sociological law"—that is, law based only on what the majority of society thinks is in its best interests at a given moment—and "sociological news," slanted to produce what some person thinks will produce a helpful sociological result. *Now arbitrary abortion has opened wide the door at the point of life and death for "sociological medicine"—not just for the yet unborn but for all human life.*

Treating Congenital Defects

The most challenging aspect of children's surgery is the treatment of those congenital defects that are incompatible with life, but nevertheless can be corrected by the proper surgical procedure carried out shortly after birth. We are talking about such defects as those in babies who are born without a connection between the throat and stomach, or with no rectum, perhaps with their abdominal organs out in the umbilical cord or up in the chest cavity, or infants with any one of a great many varieties of intestinal obstruction. Many of those babies are operated on as youngsters and grow into adult life, marry, and have children of their own.

Of course there are problems in raising some of these children, and they may on occasion constitute a burden for the rest of the family. One of us has had thirty-five years' experience in performing thousands of just such operations. No family has ever asked, "Why did you work so hard to save the life of my child?" No grown child or young adult has ever asked, "Why did you struggle so hard when you knew the outcome would not be perfect?"[40]

One of us operated at Philadelphia's Children's Hospital on young Christopher Wall, who was born with *ectopia cordis* (the heart outside the chest), actually performing fifteen different procedures over 1,117 days to get his heart repositioned without crowding and to permit his lungs to function adequately. Chris is the first patient who has ever survived after being born with this type of *ectopia cordis*. The case of Chris Wall raises a number of questions asked from time to time: "Why do you think it's right to spend that much money in caring for one child, when you could take the same amount of money and spread it over the treatment of many children?" Or, as some people asked, "What kind of life is the child living? He is on a respirator; he has never been home; his parents have almost no relationship with this son who is more emotionally tied to the nurses who have raised him during the past two years."[41] *Note:* Chris did go home after 1,117 days in the hospital and is off the respirator for as long as eight hours at a time and will eventually come off the respirator completely. A doctor is responsible to God for the manner in which he works to save a single human life. It is a matter of stewardship. The surgeon is accountable for the way he uses the gifts that God has given him. He is also responsible for the life entrusted to his care. It is a question of moral principle.

But even if we were pragmatists, we would still believe that doctors should work to save the Chris Walls of this world. For when a hospital is geared to save lives at any cost, this attitude affects health care down to the most mundane level.[42] On the other hand, when one set of patients can be eliminated at will, the whole spirit of struggling to save lives is lost, and it is not long before a doctor or nurse will say, "Why try so hard on anybody? After all, we deliberately fail to treat some patients and we kill others." Even if it were not expressed this blatantly, an erosion takes place, which over a number of years would undermine the care of all patients in any institution that kills any patient placed in its care.

Eventually, abortion must surely have this effect on the field of obstetrics. We do not understand how an obstetrician can destroy a 1000-gram fetus in one uterus and deliver a 1500-gram premature baby from out of another uterus, carrying it to the tender, loving care of the intensive-care nursery down the hall.

Just as child abuse has risen dramatically during the years of legalized abortion, the gradual brutalizing of society that is taking place has included doctors and legislators as well as ordinary citizens. If you doubt that we are becoming brutal, consider for a moment that many pediatric surgeons, highly skilled in surgery of the newborn and most knowledgeable about what can be accomplished by rehabilitation, choose not to operate on a given newborn with a given congenital defect. By making the decision of allowing him to die or acquiescing to the parents' wishes not to operate, they allow the baby to die.[43] Think of mothers who express the idea of "personal rights" by having dragged piecemeal from their wombs the child they have conceived. Think of legislators debating, as if they were talking about the price of coffee, what action they should take to eliminate economic burdens on society by opening the doors to a lack of protection for the weak, the old, the infirm, the young and the unborn—in fact, for all those our society traditionally has protected. Indeed, this protection was once a hallmark of our civilization. *Whatever happened to the human race?*

Advocates of Infanticide

It frightens us when we see the medical profession acquiesce to, if not lead in, a trend which in our judgment will carry us to destruction. The loss of humanness shown in allowing malformed babies to starve to death is not a thing of the future. It is being put forward as the accepted thing right now in many quarters. All that is left is for it to become totally accepted and eventually, for economic reasons, made mandatory by an increasingly authoritarian government in an increasingly selfish society.

In May 1973, James D. Watson, the Nobel Prize laureate who discovered the double helix of DNA, granted an interview to *Prism* magazine, then a publication of the American Medical Association. *Time* later reported the interview to the general public, quoting Watson as having said, "If a child were not declared alive until three days after birth, then all parents could be allowed the choice only a few are given under the present system. The doctor could allow the child to die if the parents so choose and save a lot of misery and suffering. I believe this view is the only rational, compassionate attitude to have."

In January 1978, Francis Crick, also a Nobel laureate, was quoted in the *Pacific News Service* as saying, ". . . no newborn infant should be declared human until it has passed certain tests regarding its genetic endowment and that if it fails these tests it forfeits the right to live."

In *Ideals of Life,* Millard S. Everett, who was professor of philosophy and humanities at Oklahoma A&M, writes, "My personal feeling—and I don't ask anyone to agree with me—is that eventually, when public opinion is prepared for it, no child should be admitted into the society of the living who would be certain to suffer any social handicap—for example, any physical or mental defect that would prevent marriage or would make others tolerate his company only from the sense of mercy." He adds, "This would imply not only eugenic sterilization but also euthanasia due to accidents of birth which cannot be foreseen."[44]

Perhaps the paper most outspokenly advocating infanticide was published in the prestigious 167-year-old *New England Journal of Medicine.* In October 1973, Dr. Raymond S. Duff and Dr. A. G. M. Campbell of the department of pediatrics at Yale University School of Medicine wrote, "Moral and Ethical Dilemmas in the Special-Care Nursery."[45]

Very few parents come of their own volition to a physician and say, "My baby has a life not worthy to be lived." Duff and Campbell say that the parents in such a case are not in a condition to give "informed consent" by themselves. But any physician in the emotional circumstances surrounding the birth of a baby with any kind of a defect can, by innuendo if not advice, prepare the family to make the decision the physician wants them to make. We do not consider this "informed consent."

Duff and Campbell acknowledge that the parents' and siblings' rights to relief from "seemingly pointless, crushing burdens were important considerations" in letting children die. Even Duff and Campbell use the word *seemingly* to modify *pointless,* and we are sure the burden would not be nearly as *crushing* as the guilt many of these parents will eventually feel.[46]

As partial justification for their point of view, Duff and Campbell say that "although some parents have exhibited doubts that the choices were correct, all appear to be as effective in their lives as they were before this experience. Some claim that their profoundly moving experience has provided a deeper meaning in life, and from this they have become more effective people." Some of the parents, the two doctors admit, had doubts that their choice to let the child die was correct. If these parents were seeking deeper meaning in life—and if Duff and Campbell were indeed interested in providing deeper meaning in life for the parents of their deformed patients—why not let the family find that deep meaning by providing the love and attention necessary to take care of an infant who has been given to them? We suspect that the deeper meaning would then be deeper still, that their effectiveness would be still more effective, and that they would be examples of courage and determination to others less courageous. Duff and Campbell say, "It seems appropriate that the profession be held accountable for presenting fully all management options and their expected consequences." We wonder how commonly physicians are willing to be held accountable for the consequences that may not be apparent in a family until years later?

There have been many times when one of us, having operated on a newborn youngster who has subsequently died, has been inwardly relieved and has expressed honestly to the family that the tragic turn of events was indeed a blessing in disguise. But being able to look on such an occasion in retrospect as a blessing does not, we believe, entitle a doctor to distribute a "shower of blessings" by eliminating the problems that families might have to face in raising a child who is less than perfect—by eliminating the baby.

On the basis of interviews he has given and comments we have read in the press, we believe that Professor Duff is perfectly sincere in believing that he is moving in an ethical and moral direction when he advocates death as one of the options in the treatment of a defective newborn. It should not be thought that we are singling out Duff and Campbell. There are growing numbers of other physicians and surgeons who unfortunately, we believe, are advocating the same course of action. Anthony Shaw, a pediatric surgeon, has been in the forefront of these discussions from a neonatal surgeon's point of view. He says: "My ethic holds that all rights are not absolute all the time. As Fletcher points out, '. . . all rights are imperfect and may be set aside if human need requires it.' My ethic further considers quality of life as a value that must be balanced against the belief in the sanctity of life."[47]

We are moving from the state of mind in which destruction of life is advocated for children who are considered to be socially useless or deemed to have nonmeaningful lives to the stance that we should perhaps destroy a child because he is socially disturbing. One wonders if the advocates of such a philosophy would espouse a total blockade and "starving out" of urban slums as a solution to poverty—considering all the social and economic problems this would solve all at once!

The twentieth century has produced many monsters. One has been the idea of "built-in obsolescence," not only in material things but also in human matters such as marriage and the responsibilities of parenthood. One can picture a parent picking up one baby and, not being quite satisfied with it, trading it in for another one.

Medical science can now make a prenatal diagnosis of the sex of the expected offspring. In spite of the depravity of our society regarding abortion-on-demand, even abortionists recoil a little from eliminating an unborn child just because it is not the sex the family wants. There was a recent example involving a couple who wanted a boy but not a girl. Rather than make this crass request of their obstetrician, they claimed to be concerned about hemophilia in the wife's family. Amniocentesis was therefore undertaken to determine the sex of the baby, because only males are affected. When the obstetrician reported that there was no need for concern because the unborn child was a girl and could not have hemophilia, the parents responded, "That's what we wanted to know. We want a boy, so now we want an abortion."

One wonders what the chances are for someone who becomes a burden in a society that practices the concept of the survival of the fittest and has begun this practice by starting to eliminate its children. Most societies, recognizing the total dependency of children, have given their young a place of special protection. Since our society has begun by abusing and then killing children, we feel that for us the worst has come first. Where the destruction will end depends only on what a small scientific elite and a generally apathetic public will advocate and tolerate. Any hope of a comprehensive standard for human rights has already been lost.

Meaningful Humanhood
Joseph Fletcher, formerly of Harvard Divinity School and now at the University of Virginia in Charlottesville, talks about "mean-

ingful humanhood" in an article entitled "Indicators of Humanhood: A Tentative Profile of Man."[48] H. Tristam Engelhart, Jr.,
formerly clinical professor of physiology of medicine at the University of Texas and more recently professor of philosophy and
medicine at the Kennedy Institute of Georgetown University in
Washington, D.C., writes of "wrongful life."[49]

As soon as we let anyone, even a physician, make decisions
about our "meaningful humanhood," about "wrongful life" or
"rightful life," we have then invited others to make decisions
about our worth. And our worth may be entirely different in the
eyes of these men or their followers from what it would have been
to anyone in our culture in the past. In fact, it might even be
different from the view held by the majority of people today.

If we decide that a child with a chronic cardiopulmonary disease, short-bowel syndrome, or various manifestations of brain
dramage should be permitted to die (some of Duff and Campbell's
examples), what is to prevent us from eliminating an adult with
chronic cardiopulmonary disease—who may be much more of a
burden to his family than the child is? Or what about an adult with
ulcerative colitis (with symptoms much the same as short-bowel
syndrome) and some psychiatric problems as well? Are we to
extend the slaughter to all those who in one way or another become a burden or nuisance, or who stop us from enjoying our
rights as we perceive them? The word *rights* is meaningless outside
the context of some moral framework that extends its protection
to the whole human family.

Because a newborn child has the possibility or even the probability of problems in later life, does this give us the right to
terminate his or her life now? If it does, then should we also do
away with the people reading this book who have chronic short-
ness of breath, oxygen dependency, paralysis, a sexual handicap,
or a psychological problem? The problems in the Duff and Campbell article all have their adult counterparts.

We think many miss the essential message in the Duff and
Campbell paper. These authors first brought to public attention
death as an option in newborn pediatric care. But it is not always
understood that the death they presented as an option *was not the
death of infants who could not possibly survive, but rather the death of
infants who could live if treated—but whose lives would not be "normal."*

The physician's decision—not the infant's defect—becomes the
lethal factor. In view of the fact that, to Duff and Campbell, the

economic status of the family and the stability of the marriage are mitigating circumstances in deciding on treatment or nontreatment, it is clear that there has been introduced a discrimination just as deplorable as those based on race, creed, color, or sex. And, as is so often the case, not only is such immoral and discriminatory behavior propagated, but those who push for it do so with high and lofty pseudomoral language.

Duff and Campbell offer death as an option in health care, even though they say in one place in their article, "We recognize great variability and often much uncertainty in prognoses and in family capacities to deal with defective newborn infants. . . . Prognosis was not always exact and a few children with extensive care might live for months and occasionally years. *Some might survive and function satisfactorily*" (italics ours).

When the physician responsible for managing a newborn baby with a defect is committed to the thesis that there is some human life not worthy to be lived, and when he considers death as one of the options in treatment, the baby concerned does not have a chance. Obviously, the determining factor is not the baby's physical defect but the physician's decision.

The *Newsweek* (November 12, 1973) report of the Duff and Campbell article quotes Duff as saying, "The public has got to decide what to do with vegetated individuals who have no human potential." This was answered by a letter in *Newsweek* two weeks later:

"Life-and-Death Decisions"

I'll wager my entire root system and as much fertilizer as it would take to fill Yale University that you have never received a letter from a vegetable before this one, but, much as I resent the term, I must confess that I fit the description of a "vegetable" as defined in the article "Shall This Child Die?"

Due to severe brain damage incurred at birth, I am unable to dress myself, toilet myself, or write; my secretary is typing this letter. Many thousands of dollars had to be spent on my rehabilitation and education in order for me to reach my present professional status as a counselling psychologist. My parents were also told, 35 years ago, that there was "little or no hope of achieving meaningful 'humanhood' " for their daughter. Have I reached "humanhood"? Compared with Drs. Duff and Campbell, I believe I have surpassed it!

Instead of changing the law to make it legal to weed out us "vegetables," let us change the laws so that we may receive quality medical care, education and freedom to live as full and productive lives as our potentials allow.

Sondra Diamond
Philadelphia, Pa.

The medical profession has traditionally made its treatment of patients a reflection of our society's concern for those who are ill or helpless. Indeed, it has often acted as an advocate for those who had no one else to stand up for them. Thus it responded, in days gone by, with love and compassion toward the helpless child. Technical skills have increased rapidly and have produced dilemmas that doctors did not face a decade ago. But this does not give them any new expertise in deciding who shall live and who shall die, especially when so many nonmedical factors must be taken into account in making the decision. The new gadgetry of medical practice and the growing sophistication of technology do not give a doctor any more right than the rest of us to play God. Many in the medical profession are losing this viewpoint. They are setting the worth of the individual person aside. We would insist that if we cannot cure, we can care; and we do not mean ever to use the words *care* and *kill* as synonyms.

Infanticide in America Today

As early as 1973, Drs. Duff and Campbell made it clear that infanticide was happening in American hospitals. From the early 1970s onward the proinfanticide advocates in this country began a concentrated assault to convince the nation that killing a newborn baby was sometimes the most compassionate course of treatment. Through articles appearing in leading medical, legal, and philosophical journals many members of the medical and legal professions became convinced that death was a valid treatment option. But much of this debate over infanticide took place away from the attention of the American public. Ordinary people remained completely unaware that such horrible options were being considered by those to whom they entrusted their children for care.

It was not until 1981 that infanticide came out of the shadows of the newborn nursery. In May of that year in Danville, Illinois, twin boys were born to a doctor and his wife. The twins were joined at the waist and shared several organs. At their birth, as a nurse later testified, their father ordered that no oxygen be given the babies and also insisted that they receive no food or water. The twins were taken to the nursery and left to starve. The boys would have died except for an anonymous phone call placed to the Department of Child and Family Services letting them know that the babies were being neglected. That call resulted in an indictment for attempted murder against the boys' parents and doctor. The charges were eventually dropped, but not before the national media had grabbed hold of the case and brought infanticide to the public's attention. The boys were transferred to another hospital and were eventually returned to their parents' custody. Today the twins, much to everyone's amazement, have been surgically separated and are progressing well at home with their parents.

The twins' case is important for several reasons. A situation like this is often referred to as a "hard case." The boys had several serious medical complications. Doctors were skeptical about the possibility of separation. Often proinfanticide advocates point to a case like this and talk about the "hopelessness" of future life for these babies. Because the case is medically complex and the situation serious, they advise simply leaving the children to die. But even in this "hard case" the twins did survive. The medical complexities were not beyond solving, and the situation was far from hopeless. No one can predict the medical future with certainty, and no one's judgment that a situation is complex or complicated should move us to kill the child.

Secondly, even though the charges were eventually dropped, this case brought out the fact that the law holds parents and doctors responsible for their decisions about their children. Both parties have a duty to care for their children. When they do not, the law punishes them. *The handicapped newborn baby is absolutely protected under the law* in the same way as a healthy adult.

This fact—that the law still protects the handicapped newborn—needs to be stressed. Infanticide is not a question of parents having the right to kill their children. Many infanticide advocates argue that the decision about a child's life should be left to the parents, in consultation with their doctor. If the parents want the baby, he lives; if not he dies. But our law has never given parents the right to kill their newborn children—and there is no exception for handicapped babies. Parents, physicians, and hospitals can be charged with a variety of crimes ranging from murder to child abuse. The amazing thing is that *more* charges have not been brought against parents and doctors who practice infanticide. That shows us just how effective proinfanticide forces have been in convincing those in medicine and the law that infanticide is okay. Even though the laws are on the books, many are allowing the courts to look the other way when it comes to handicapped newborn babies and parents' decisions not to treat them.

Even more well-known than the twins' case is the tragic death of Infant Doe in Bloomington, Indiana. In 1982 a baby boy known only as Baby Doe was born to parents in that city. The child had Down's syndrome and a badly formed esophagus. The esophageal problem was easily correctable by a routinely performed operation. Yet, because their son was handicapped, the parents refused permission to operate. They also ordered that their son be given no food or water. Two Indiana courts hailed their decision. The child's pediatricians pleaded with the parents to let their child live, and to allow them to operate. They pointed out that persons with Down's syndrome had happy and productive lives. Other Indiana couples offered to adopt the baby if the parents didn't want him. Lawyers for Baby Doe prepared to appeal the Indiana courts' decision. Yet the parents would not be moved. Seven days later, as the baby's lawyers were en route to the U.S. Supreme Court to launch an appeal, Baby Doe died. It was a cruel and painful death by starvation.

This was a case that outraged the nation. Newspaper columnists and national commentators condemned this horrible act. President Reagan expressed his sorrow and anger at Baby Doe's death. In Congress the Hon. Henry Hyde spoke about this little child who died "because there just wasn't enough love to go around."

Baby Doe's death was a clear-cut case of infanticide. His parents did not want him to live because he was handicapped. In their opinion his life was not worth living. Acting in response to this case and several other similar cases that soon came to light, the Department of Health and Human Services issued a regulation in March 1983 informing hospitals of their duty to treat handicapped children. The regulation warned that hospitals could lose their federal funding for failure to treat all children equally. In addition they provided a "hotline" number that people could call when they felt a child was being neglected. This was an unprecedented move by the government and one that will protect the lives of thousands of handicapped children.

But the battle against legalized infanticide is far from ended. The American Academy of Pediatrics, along with several other organizations, has filed suit against the HHS ruling. They claim that the law should not interfere with the practice of medicine, and that parents should have the right to decide their child's fate. But this ruling does not interfere with a doctor's decisions as long as he is making a decision based on his best *medical* judgment, and not on his opinion about the child's quality of life. When doctors stay within their field of expertise the law protects them. If a doctor believes that, in his best judgment, there is no treatment that can improve the child's chances for life, or that there are so many handicaps that the case is medically hopeless, then he cannot be prosecuted under the law. But if a doctor decides not to treat a child simply because the child is handicapped and he believes the child's life is "worthless," then he is acting outside his area of medical expertise. He is making quality of life judgments, and the law must act to protect the child.

Many times proinfanticide advocates in medicine and the media claim that these cases are too complex to be decided by a simple regulation. But often this cry of complexity is a smoke screen to hide the doctor's true intent. Look at the most publicized infanticide cases—the Johns Hopkins baby, Baby Doe, and the Danville twins. These were not cases that were too complex to allow the children to live. The first two cases involved a simple, routinely performed operation to save the child's life. Both these children had Down's syndrome—a fairly common handicap that is certainly *not* incompatible with life. The operation was denied them *only because they were handicapped.* They were starved to death simply because their lives didn't measure up to someone else's arbitrary standard. In the case of the twins, their situation presented many medical complexities. But the decision not to feed the boys was not based on any medical factors. That decision was made before any medical information was available, and it was based solely on the fact that they were handicapped. As it turned out, the medical complexities could be overcome and the boys could be separated. We must not allow ourselves to be persuaded that infanticide is too complex an issue to be decided by the law: the children who are being "allowed to die" in our hospitals are very rarely "hopeless" cases.

We cannot underestimate the enormity of the battle before us. For over a decade proinfanticide forces have been preparing us to accept legalized infanticide. Legalized abortion has made infanticide the next logical step in the devaluation and destruction of innocent lives. Technology such as amniocentesis and ultrasound has enabled us to diagnose a variety of handicaps in the womb. We can legally kill a handicapped child or any child up until the day it is born. But what is the difference between killing a child two days before it is born or two days after its birth? The proinfanticide forces are also using the same methods now that the proabortion advocates used to see abortion legalized. That is, they now focus on the "hard cases" in a way that opens the door. Later, as has happened in abortion, these "hard cases" will be forgotten as infanticide becomes normal practice.

It is ironic that it is medicine that in this age of science has turned back the clock and begun using the most primitive solution to social problems of all, death. So much for the "healing art."

Infanticide and the Church

Mauthausen in Austria was a Nazi concentration camp where, between 1938 and 1945, over 110,000 people were brutally killed to help build the Nazis' idea of heaven on earth. There are monuments to the many Jews and non-Jews who died. What happened in Mauthausen shows the lowest possible view of human life. All conventions of war were put aside, as people of all nationalities were tortured and had pseudomedical experiments performed on them.

To the Nazis the Jews were an unwanted burden on society—parasites who consumed more than they gave. The young, the old, the aged, the weak, and the strong were all eliminated in an attempt to build a perfect race according to Nazi standards. Individuals were no longer perceived as special creatures created in the image of God. Regardless of their nationality or race, people were viewed as pawns to be exploited, and when they no longer fulfilled a function, they were eliminated.

Not so long ago, at the Charleston, South Carolina, slave market, black men, women, and children were sold as cattle. On a balcony they were paraded as so much merchandise before the prospective buyers standing down below. For economic convenience, they had been arbitrarily reclassified by a white society as nonhuman. The Supreme Court of the United States, in the Dred Scott Decision, upheld this fiction by declaring the black person to be chattel property.

These atrocities are not just a record in past history. There is in our own day a low view of human life, not only in the secular world but in certain religious groups as well. The Religious Coalition for Abortion Rights is a case in point. Among what the organization calls its "eleven major denominations" are the Unitarian Universal Association, the American Ethical Union, the American Jewish Congress, and the Union of American Hebrew Congregations. This group has attempted to use anti-Catholic thinking as a weapon by declaring that abortion is a Roman Catholic issue. Its position on abortion is weakened by ignorance—because it seeks the "legal option of abortion in accordance with sound medical practice." Actually, this "sound medical practice" is just the whim of the mother-to-be.

Dean J. Philip Wogaman of Wesley Theological Seminary has espoused the cause of the Religious Coalition for Abortion Rights by ignoring the right of the developing, unborn baby in favor of what he calls "God's loving intention for existing human beings."[50] That "loving intention" for an existing human being turns out to be supporting the mother-to-be in the murder of her unborn child.

Certain segments of the church are also not without a positive opinion on the subject of infanticide. A task force of the Anglican Church of Canada reached a conclusion in a 1977 report that it could be morally right to terminate the lives of newborn infants with severe brain damage. The callousness of the report is evident in its phraseology: "Our sense and emotions lead us to the grave mistake of treating human-looking shapes as if they were human, although they lack the least vestige of human behavior and intellect. In fact the only way to treat such defective infants humanely is not to treat them as human."[51]

The task force was made up of eleven people with backgrounds in medicine, nursing, law, and theology. It is astounding that the professions represented could have produced such a report. It is humanism producing inhumanity. The self-assured language of these individuals and people like them must surely remind us of the words and sentiments expressed by those who in another era were espousing and defending slavery and attempting to prove the nonhuman status of the black person.

Happily, the general synod of the Anglican Church in Canada did not approve the report, but that such a report came forth from an official group of a major denomination in our day says much about the direction taken by certain segments of the church in regard to infanticide.

That even the church is being used by the proponents of infanticide is particularly alarming. Those who have propagated these ideas or simply not bothered to think them through have had ample warning in history—if they would care to look. Doctors and nurses should be aware of how fallible these decisions are and how disastrous have been simplistic pop-science theories about human worth in the past. Lawyers should be frightened to let down the bars on the killing of any human being, when the decision is made on the arbitrary basis of the quality of life. And finally, these theologians have obviously forgotten God's view of the worth of every human being as made in the image of God. If these same theologians no longer believe in such a God, they should not use the church as a platform from which to propagate their discriminatory ideas.

In general, liberal theologians and church bodies (those who have tried to mix Christian and humanistic thought) support abortion and thus contribute to the subsequent slide into the loss of humanness. These religious groups have departed from the stand against abortion that the Christian church has taken from its earliest days. The *Didache,* or *The Teaching of the Twelve Apostles,* an early Christian document from the second century (or maybe even the late first century) clearly prohibits abortion. Tertullian, in his *Apologeticus* of A.D. 197 writes:

> For us murder is once for all forbidden; so even the child in the womb, while yet the mother's blood is still being drawn on to form the human being, it is not lawful for us to destroy. To forbid birth is only quicker murder. It makes no difference whether one take away the life once born or destroy it as it comes to birth. He is a man, who is to be a man; the fruit is always present in the seed.

Those in the church who have not made these questions a burning issue have forgotten the church's centuries-old tradition of social action on behalf of the weak and the unwanted. One remembers William Wilberforce, fighting the slave trade in the British Empire on the basis of his Christian faith, representative of the many down through the ages who have tried to practice what they preach.

What Chance for Humanity?

At a population-control conference in Washington, D.C., as reported by editor-writer Norman Podhoretz, one speaker saw "no reason why anyone who accepted abortion should balk at infanticide." Another urged certain medical qualifying tests for all newborns. These would determine their genetic characteristics and, thus, whether their right to life should be forfeited.[52] Of course, at present only a few hold these ideas, but unfortunately they are presenting these ideas again and again. Taken a little more seriously each time, they become just a little more thinkable each time.

Link this view with the abuse of genetic knowledge, the ever-expanding power of the government, and arbitrary law, and, indeed, the prospects for the right of the individual and for humanness are grim. Dr. James R. Sorenson, associate professor of socio-medical sciences at Boston University Medical Center, spoke at the symposium "Prenatal Diagnosis and Its Impact on Society" and said:

> [There is] a developing cultural or social attitude that . . . a couple ought to exercise control over their reproductive fate. While a couple should have as many children as they please (within cultural "limits"), increasingly our societal view is that they should not have unwanted children. I think that this developing societal attitude can very easily extend to encompass not just control of the number of children but . . . control of their quality as well. In short, I am suggesting that it may become culturally acceptable and perhaps even expected that parents ought to avoid the birth of a defective child, especially when we have a technology that can help avoid such events.

The matter does not stop with malformed babies, but leads naturally to limiting the number of babies a family may have. In 1971, at the National Conference on Population Education in Washington, D.C., Martha Willing, codirector of Population Dynamics of Seattle, Washington, first proposed tax disincentives for parents who have more than two children. Then the state should proceed "to penalize deliberate violations of a small family norm and set up controls which prevent such violations." The author continues:

> After the third child is born, both mother and father will have to present themselves at a hospital to undergo sterilization procedures. If the couple does not appear, there will be no birth certificate issued to the third child, but instead a "third child paper." The mother can be tattooed or marked to signify a third birth to any subsequent doctor. Instead of the missing parent, the child can be sterilized on the spot, insuring that this undue share of the gene pool will not be carried forward.[53]

Without the Judeo-Christian base which gives every individual an intrinsic dignity as made in the image of the personal-infinite Creator, each successive horror falls naturally into place. Combine arbitrary law (in which a small group of people may decide what is good for society at that moment of history) with the Supreme Court ruling on arbitrary abortion and the gates are opened for many kinds of killing under the guise of social good. Nan Mizrachi, in "Eliminating the Medical Hazards of Delayed Abortions," says:

> Arguments that the fetus is only "human" at a particular stage of gestation violate biological reality. It attempts to oversimplify a complex issue. Whereas the reality that abortion is killing should not, in my view, remove abortion as a socially acceptable surgical procedure, I do think we should face up to the reality of what the decision to abort entails.[54]

In other words, abortion is killing, but it is nevertheless to be practiced. But if that kind of killing, why not others?

As much as we would differ with Professor Joseph Fletcher's views of ethics, we can agree that his logic is impeccable when he says in *The Humanist* (July-August 1974): "To speak of living and dying, therefore . . . encompasses the abortion issue along with the euthanasia issue. They are ethically inseparable."

Here we come to the next logical step that follows from abandoning the biblical perspective that mankind is unique, in that all men, women, and children are made in the image of God. The wide-open door of abortion-on-demand leads naturally to infanticide which leads naturally to euthanasia.

CHAPTER THREE

Death by Someone's Choice

Life is a continuum from conception until natural death. Since life is being destroyed before birth, why not tamper with it on the other end?

Will a society which has assumed the right to kill infants in the womb—because they are unwanted, imperfect, or merely inconvenient—have difficulty in assuming the right to kill other human beings, especially older adults who are judged unwanted, deemed imperfect physically or mentally, or considered a possible social nuisance?

The next candidates for arbitrary reclassification as nonpersons are the elderly. This will become increasingly so as the proportion of the old and weak in relation to the young and strong becomes abnormally large, due to the growing antifamily sentiment, the abortion rate, and medicine's contribution to the lengthening of the normal life span. The imbalance will cause many of the young to perceive the old as a cramping nuisance in the hedonistic lifestyle they claim as their right. As the demand for affluence continues and the economic crunch gets greater, the amount of compassion that the legislature and the courts will have for the old does not seem likely to be significant considering the precedent of the nonprotection given to the unborn and newborn.

How did the concept of euthanasia get such a head start in the seventies? We must keep referring back to abortion—because it is the Supreme Court decision on abortion that stated that "only viable human beings who have the capability for meaningful life may, but need not, be protected by the state." That statement could be a death warrant for many in a few years.

Euthanasia: "Death with Dignity"

The word *euthanasia* becomes a respectable part of our vocabulary and consciousness in a subtle way, via the phrase *death with dignity*. This term was first used, as far as we know, in a book published in Germany in 1920 by Karl Binding and Alfred Hoche: *The Release of the Destruction of Life Devoid of Value.*[55] There is no doubt about what the authors meant by the term. They made it the motto of the movement to legalize the killing of a person who had "the right to the complete relief of an unbearable life." *But,* we have to ask, *"unbearable" by whose definition?*

Starving to death a newborn infant with a congenital defect is given the name *passive euthanasia,* and somehow or other seems more acceptable in the minds of those who commit such an atrocity than taking an active step to kill the same child.

On occasion, a physician may decide to withhold extraordinary means in the management of a patient. Is there ever justification for this? First of all, one must define the term *extraordinary* as it refers to medical care. Things which are extraordinary today will not be extraordinary next year, and things which were extraordinary last year are ordinary now. There was a day when the administration of oxygen or the use of intravenous fluids was extraordinary—and so it has been with respirators, pacemakers, and heart-lung machines.

One of us has shown that newborns with severe congenital defects (those incompatible with life) upon whom he operates would *ordinarily* never survive—without extraordinary care. Yet, with that extraordinary care, most live and grow and do well without the continuation of any of the extraordinary measures. As a Christian, does this surgeon have any guidelines? For him it comes down to a matter of stewardship. He is answerable to society for the skills he exercises in the care of his patients. Yet, above that, he believes that he is also answerable to God for the skills he has been given, as well as for the care of the patients God has entrusted to him.

To use nonreligious terms, the issue is motivation. It is his motivation or intent that a physician must keep uppermost in his mind. He must constantly be aware of the wonderful uniqueness of human life. Of course, at times he faces difficult decisions. Once he believes that the technical gadgetry he is using is merely prolonging the experience of dying, rather than extending life, he can withdraw the extraordinary means and let nature take its course, while keeping the patient as comfortable as possible. This is what physicians have done for years, in the realm of trust between patient and physician or between the patient's family and physician. That is truly "death with dignity," and no mere manufactured euphemism for euthanasia.

This is not the question being debated today, however. It is not doctors with a biblical view of life who are debating the cases in which death is imminent and inevitable. Rather, it is a whole new breed of medical and paramedical personnel for whom the issues go much further. With these individuals, the intent is to advocate the death of a patient either by directly killing him, or by doing nothing when there could be given help and support that would result in life—even though the circumstances might be difficult. This, ironically, is called "mercy killing."

The next step is to destroy human individuals or groups of individuals because they are unwanted, imperfect, or socially embarrassing. Senility, infirmity, retardation, insanity, and incontinence are conditions that come to mind. Obviously, when one comes to that practice, he has gone far beyond even so-called mercy killing. He has entered the same realm as that of Nazi behavior during World War II. This is essentially what abortionists are doing with unborn babies—because many of these abortionists have no medical concern for whether the unborn babies live. To have those babies is merely inconvenient, uneconomical, or perhaps embarrassing. Carrying this practice to its logical conclusion, we come to death selection and genocide.

The Case of Karen Quinlan

When one discusses euthanasia, the case of Karen Quinlan comes to mind as probably the best-known medical-ethical dilemma of recent years. To summarize very briefly: Karen Quinlan was delivered to an emergency room of a community hospital by friends.

She was unconscious after having taken a combination of alcohol and drugs. If a thousand people were delivered to an emergency room in such a condition, the result would probably be a few survivors and a tremendous number of deaths, but Karen Quinlan lived on in an unconscious limbo between life and death.

Miss Quinlan was undoubtedly in a most deplorable physical state. She lost a great deal of weight and lay in a fetal position. Although she was unconscious, she was far from legally dead. She responded to pain and noise and withdrew her limbs when they were stroked. Expert medical witnesses from various parts of the country said that she would never recover and that her life was being sustained only by the mechanical respirator which breathed for her. Because of this "expert testimony," Karen's parents petitioned the court to direct the physicians caring for their daughter to "pull the plug" on the respirator. Judge Robert Muir, Jr., of the lower New Jersey court delivered a remarkable verdict, which ruled that to disconnect the respirator would be an act of homicide, because Karen would be unable to support her own respiratory effort and would die.[56]

Subsequently, Karen's family appealed this decision to the Supreme Court of New Jersey, which reversed the lower court's decision. These judges said that the plug *could* be pulled.[57] Accordingly, the respirator was disconnected, and—to everyone's amazement—Karen went right on breathing. This should be a lesson for all concerned. Medical opinion, no matter how learned and expert, is never infallible.[58]

If Judge Muir in Morristown, New Jersey, had ruled that the plug could be pulled in this case, it would have been legitimate for other patients in the same condition as Karen to be candidates for the same kind of treatment. At the time of Judge Muir's decision, one of us had under his care four children who did not match all the neurological criteria of Karen Quinlan, but who were unconscious, though responsive to loud noises and pain, and had all their respiratory needs cared for by mechanical respirators. If Judge Muir had said to remove Karen's respirator, it might have been logical for the hospital's administrator, medical staff, nursing personnel, or the parents of these patients to have said, "Look, there is now a legal precedent. Let's disconnect the machines and get this over with." But all these children eventually went home well. It is obvious that one cannot accept the same legal guidelines for all people, not even when there is a court trial, expert testimony, and every other indicator that says, "Do it this way and it will be all right."[59]

Does Anyone Want to Die?

The concern about euthanasia and the use of that term in our common vocabulary lead to a degradation of the elderly and, ultimately, to inferior health care for the elderly—as well as encouraging the thought that those who do not want to "shuffle off" quickly are somehow failing in their contribution to society. Economic considerations then creep in, and old folks are made to feel—in this crazy, schizophrenic society of ours—that they are in some way depriving younger and more deserving people of the medical care that is now being provided them at the same cost. For example, one of the undersecretaries of the Department of Health, Education and Welfare suggested in 1977 that the various states that did not enact living-will legislation be penalized by having withdrawn or curtailed the federal funds that would ordinarily supplement state funds allocated for certain major programs.[60]

Some people not only believe that men and women are only machines, but are acting on the idea that they are only so many digits in one big computer. Feelings that place warmth, love, and compassion—not to mention the beauty and reality of human relationships—above other considerations are often all put aside for the great god of efficiency, especially in the economic realm.

We must be careful not to be misled by the euthanasia forces. They are active as they have never been before. Consider, for example, the following statement under the heading "The Right to Choose Death" by Professor O. Ruth Russell (*The New York Times*, February 14, 1972): "Surely it is time to ask why thousands of dying, incurable and senile persons are being kept alive—sometimes by massive blood transfusions, intravenous feedings, artificial respiration and other heroic measures—who unmistakably want to die." There are thousands of "dying, incurable and senile persons" who are alive—not through any extraordinary means, but just plain "alive." When Dr. Russell says that some "unmistakably want to die," how does she know that if an appreciable number of these people could be helped to live, they would not be exceedingly grateful for all that had been done to keep them alive? Many of us have heard people say, "I want to die"—even those without great pain—and find that only a short time later they think completely differently about living.

There are put forward so many arguments, using such terms as "rights" and "compassion." These terms are borrowed from a more moral and compassionate age, and their use is purely manipulative and deceptive, because the words can cover the most barbarous ideas with a certain emotional respectability. When these ideas gain acceptance, the results are ugly. The original so-called ideal is soon forgotten and traded in for pragmatic, arbitrary, and economic factors. And the situation becomes more and more brutal and careless of life, people, individuality, and humanness.

Dr. Malcolm Todd, president-elect of the American Medical Association in 1973, argued that physicians should not have to make the decisions on mercy killings by themselves, even if they are merely decisions to refrain from medical intervention. He suggested that the needed determinations be made by boards made up of diverse kinds of people. Do you see what this would bring to the scene? This board would be merely a way of spreading the decision-making responsibility to many so-called experts, who would each decide on the basis of the criteria of his own field.

Such a broad review does not establish a solid base for either objectivity or morality. All you would need is someone convinced that too much money is being spent on elderly people—and what started as a board to decide on extraordinary means could quickly become a death-selection committee, if it lacked objectivity and moral criteria.[61]

When Dr. Philip H. Addison was secretary of the Medical Defense Union in London, the British Medical Association Board of Science and Education told the Third World Congress on Medical Law, meeting in Ghent, Belgium, that dying patients seldom ask for euthanasia. Those knowing that they are dying usually welcome any prolongation of life. The report went on to say that the majority of deaths in the present day can be made peaceful, whatever the nature and character of the preceding illness. It has been said that modern medicine can now overcome pain without shortening life. If this is really so, the case for legalizing euthanasia is considerably weakened.[62]

Thus we find that the pragmatic arguments for euthanasia are often based on a world-view which holds a low opinion of life, rather than being grounded on facts. Even if some token willingness on the part of the prospective euthanasia victim is prescribed as a criterion—in this day of manipulation and the vast potential for the like-minded media to put pressure on people—what real choice will the potential victim have, especially if he or she is ill and in pain?

Another argument for euthanasia is given by Joseph Fletcher, the popularizer of "situational ethics," in his 1973 discussion of death with dignity in the *American Journal of Nursing*:

> It is ridiculous to give ethical approval to the positive ending of sub-human life in utero as we do in therapeutic abortions for reasons of mercy and compassion but refuse to approve of positively ending a sub-human life in extremis. If we are morally obliged to put an end to a pregnancy when an amniocentesis reveals a terribly defective fetus, we are equally obliged to put an end to a patient's hopeless misery when a brain scan reveals that a patient with cancer has advanced brain metastases.[63]

Fletcher declares without discussion that ethical approval has been given to ending the lives of babies out of "compassion." Then he puts that very questionable "ethical approval" in the form of an obligation and says that because we are obliged to do that, we are also morally obliged to put an end to the life of a patient who has cancer with advanced brain metastases. To argue otherwise, he says, is ridiculous.[64]

Thus, once again, the most deplorable sentiments are presented in the guise of some humanitarian gesture. One is reminded of the slaveholders who devoutly espoused the theory that slavery was really for the good of the black man and that in the end he would be thankful for the opportunity to share the white man's culture, even from the distance of the garden shed! The Nazis also argued that their victims were being sacrificed for the high end of the general good of society. We look upon such people as Joseph Fletcher as great meddlers in human lives. They are also meddlers in God's business.

Euthanasia and the Law
Much of what is happening in the area of euthanasia is taking place in our courts. We may not hear much about the subject in the press, but each time a decision is made in a case a legal precedent is set. In the past several years our courts have set many legal precedents and had much to say on the subjects of euthanasia, termination of treatment, and the right to die. As John Whitehead has pointed out in *The Second American Revolution*, when we understand what has been happening in the courtroom, we will under-

stand just how easily legalized euthanasia could come to America.

Our law currently gives an adult a right to refuse medical treatment, especially when the treatment is extraordinary and the patient is suffering from a terminal illness. No one can force a competent adult to take a treatment unless the state believes that it has a greater interest in preserving the life of the person. The right to refuse treatment has always been part of what is known as the common law.

But in the Karen Quinlan case the courts went beyond the *common law right* to refuse treatment and spoke of a new so-called *constitutional right* to privacy, which included the right to refuse unwanted treatment. In a later case a Massachusetts court ruled that if a patient was unable to exercise this newfound constitutional right another person could be appointed to make that decision for him. In other words, someone else could decide if the person should live or die.

When the Quinlan court spoke of a constitutional right to refuse treatment, it opened the door for abuse of that right and helped pave the way for legalized euthanasia in America. A constitutional right is much broader and open to greater interpretation than a common law right. The common law already recognized a right to refuse treatment. But when such a right is said to be part of the Constitution, courts begin developing their own interpretations of what that right means.

In 1973 the Supreme Court found a new constitutional right to privacy. In their interpretation, that right inexplicably included the right to have an abortion. So when courts begin to interpret constitutional rights, no one can predict the outcome.

This expansion of a constitutional right is exactly what happened in a case in New York known as the Brother Fox case. Here the court ruled that a person has a constitutional right to die with dignity. But they went further to say that even if the patient had not indicated that he wanted treatment withheld someone else could make a "substituted judgment" for the person and have the treatment removed. Someone else could exercise *your* right to die, and bring on your death.

Notice that in this case the court did not talk about a right to refuse treatment. It talked about a much stronger and action-taking right—the right to die. This change in wording is important. The right to die can be another set of code words for legalized euthanasia. If everyone has a right to die then they also have a right to end their lives (or have someone else do it for them) by direct or indirect means. This is no longer a case of someone simply deciding that they want to refuse a costly and painful treatment that will only prolong the dying process. This was a case of a court creating a new legal right to die that could easily be interpreted to mean legalized euthanasia.

Fortunately, the case went to a higher court. There the judges ruled on it without referring to any constitutional right to die. In their opinion the law was clear enough already, and there was no need to create a new and complex constitutional right.

The Brother Fox case should serve as a warning to us for several reasons. It reveals to us just how subtly legalized euthanasia could be instituted in our nation. One court creates a new constitutional right. The next court expands on that right, and in a very short time we are able to legally kill our elderly, infirm, and anyone else who doesn't measure up to our standards of perfection. Just as legalized abortion came to us through a single decision by the U.S. Supreme Court, so too could euthanasia be legalized through the quick deliberations of a judge.

Secondly, this case warns us about the use of language. Language is an important tool in convincing others of your position. Euthanasia advocates have been skillful in masking their true intent with slogans like "death with dignity" and "a right to die." These phrases easily capture people's attention. Everyone believes in a death with dignity. But these slogans take on new meaning when they are interpreted by our courts. The right to die may sound wonderful—until we realize that legally it means that you can kill yourself or someone can kill you, even if you don't want to die. Language is powerful. But when it is interpreted by the courts it becomes much more than mere slogans. It becomes the law of the land, and often that interpretation is not at all what we expected. We must not be manipulated into accepting euthanasia because of the clever use of words and ideas that play upon our compassion. The proeuthanasia forces in our nation have purposely chosen these slogans to mask their true intent. They realize that the American public is not ready to accept legalized euthanasia, and they also realize the power of the courts in this area. Proabortionists realized that the courts were their only hope of legalizing abortion. Proinfanticide advocates also realize the important role the courts will play. While they soothe our fears with sugarcoated rhetoric, they are working hard in the judicial system to realize their goal of death by someone's choice.

Reports in the Press

With arbitrary abortion already declared legal, the speed with which the other forms of killing are being accepted must take even their advocates by surprise. The medical and scientific professions are not the only culprits. Popular apathy in general and small negatively active groups in particular have contributed much to the demise of the unique worth of humanity. Members of the government as well as the press have also shut their eyes or simply drifted along, having no firm moral base themselves. But the main culprit is the humanistic consensus, which declares man to be a machine and demotes his unique worth in his own eyes.

Let us examine a few of the discussions of euthanasia in the media. The Associated Press reports: DEBATE RAGES IN EN-GLAND OVER "DEATH PILL FOR AGED." A British doctor, John Goundry, says that a "death pill" will be available and perhaps obligatory by the end of the century. He says that doctors should be able to give a "demise pill" to old people if they ask for it. He also says, "In the end I can see the state taking over and insisting on euthanasia."[65]

David Hobman, director of Help the Aged in Britain, has said that the suggestion of a death pill seems to him totally inconsistent with the Hippocratic Oath. This oath has already been changed (*see* note 3 for chapter 1), and as there is increasing loss of humanness we can expect to see it changed even more radically.

Swedish public-health physician Ragnar Toss wants to open a suicide clinic for the more than 2,000 Swedes who kill themselves each year—"not to treat them but to help them do it." Dr. Toss, writing in the respected *Swedish Medical Journal* of August 1977, says that this suggestion is related to the choice that women now have about abortions.

So you see, this is not just theory for the future. As people are confronted with the flow of ideas from arbitrary abortion to infanticide to euthanasia, "death by someone's choice" becomes increasingly thinkable. The case of a woman in Great Britain is an illustration of the drift to the thinkableness of abortion/infanticide/euthanasia—all part of the natural trend toward the loss of humanness. Yolande McShane urged her mother in a nursing home to take an overdose of sleeping pills that she had brought her. The mother, showing attitudes rooted in Christianity, resisted: "A dog hasn't got a soul. I'm so afraid of being punished after. It's a mortal sin." The daughter gave the answer which the erosion of the Christian base and the consequent loss of humanness would naturally produce: "People are doing it left, right and center. It's not a sin anymore—it's nothing nowadays."[66]

Of course, if a human being is *not* made in the image of God, why shouldn't the malformed young and the elderly be put out of the way for the good of society—once society and the courts separate life and personhood? "Right" or "wrong" is then only a matter of what the majority thinks at that given moment, or what the courts judge is for the benefit of society at that moment. The next turn of the screw comes quickly, when a noble-sounding phrase like "the good of society" is replaced by cold, hard economics. Yolande McShane's case is apt in this regard. She was in debt and, had her attempt at euthanasia been successful, would have inherited a considerable sum from her mother's will.

According to a news report, the doctor in England who advocated the "death pill"—and said that he could see the state's insisting on euthanasia—also built his argument on economics. "[Dr. John] Goundry said hundreds of British hospitals have been taken over to house the aged sick and that hotels once serving the rich now house the old. The economics are devastating."[67]

If you say that this is just the idea of one man, think again. What is the new element in the United States' debate regarding abortion? It is sheer economics. A *Newsweek* article was titled "Abortion: Who Pays?" This article dealt with a June 20, 1977, Supreme Court ruling on abortion funding. With the Christian consensus on abortion thrown out, the argument slides into the issue of which will cost society more—free abortions or caring for the babies who are born. *Newsweek* reports: "According to HEW estimates, the price of a Medicaid abortion in the first trimester is $150, while the first year cost to taxpayers of each unwanted child is $2,200."[68] This figure, of course, fails to take into consideration the fact that many children who are unwanted in the first months of pregnancy are wanted and loved after they are born, and thus do not become an economic burden on society. Justice Lewis Powell wrote one of the majority opinions on the 1977 Supreme Court ruling that stated that the individual states may not ban abortions, but that they do not necessarily have to pay for them. Powell also added a footnote: "Legitimate demographic concerns . . . could constitute a substantial reason for departure from a position of neutrality between abortion and childbirth." These "legitimate demographic concerns" mean that the government could give free abortions in one place and deny them in another, in order to increase population in the one location, while holding it down in the other.

Or it could mean that the government could give free abortions to one class of people or one race and deny it to another, in order to change the mix of the population. How could anyone read this footnote by a Supreme Court Justice and not be startled and incensed at the doors it opens for government manipulation and for a further thrust of dehumanization? Here again, with morals in law gone, we are left with the harsh and ugly linkage of economics and manipulation.

The Holocaust
Does all this still seem an extreme projection? The fork is three-pronged: first, arbitrary sociological law by the courts and legislators; second, the changed attitude of the medical profession; third, the general apathy and selfishness of the population, which in the name of "rights" grasps at a more and more hedonistic life-style.

Recent history has something to teach us about where we are. We think historians are becoming aware that a great number of the abnormal behavior patterns of man were concentrated in the Nazi experience. Richard L. Rubenstein, in his book *The Cunning of History: Mass Death and the American Future,* speaks of the Holocaust in this way:

> The destruction process required the cooperation of every sector of German society. The bureaucrats drew the definitions and decrees, the churches gave evidence of Aryan descent, the postal authorities carried the messages of definition, expropriation, denaturalization and deportation. A place [of execution was] made available to the Gestapo and the SS by the Wehrmacht. To repeat, the operation required and received the participation of every major social and political and religious institution of the German Reich.[69]

The important thing to remember is that the medical profession took a leading part in the planning of abortion and euthanasia. It seems likely that had it not been for the example and active role played by German physicians in the practice of euthanasia, Hitler's progress in the extermination programs would have been slowed if not stopped. The medical profession went along with Nazism in discouragingly large numbers. More than a few participated in the terror, genocide, extermination programs, and active and barbaric experimentation on the unfortunate minorities in the Nazi grip.[70]

In 1946 and 1947, Leo Alexander, a Boston psychiatrist, was

consultant to the Secretary of War and on duty with the office of Chief of Counsel for War Crimes in Nuremberg. In a remarkable paper, "Medical Science Under Dictatorship," he outlined the problem. His concerns were vital when he first wrote about them in this country in 1949; they are of even greater concern to us today. Here are some of the highlights of Dr. Alexander's presentation:

> Irrespective of other ideological trappings, the guiding philosophic principle of recent dictatorships, including that of the Nazis, has been Hegelian in that what has been considered "rational utility" and corresponding doctrine and planning has replaced moral, ethical and religious values. . . .
>
> Medical science in Nazi Germany collaborated with this Hegelian trend particularly in the following enterprises: the mass extermination of the chronically sick in the interest of saving "useless" expenses to the community as a whole; the mass extermination of those considered socially disturbing or racially and ideologically unwanted; the individual, inconspicuous extermination of those considered disloyal within the ruling group; and the ruthless use of "human experimental material" for medico-military research. . . .
>
> It started with the acceptance of the attitude basic in the euthanasia movement, that there is such a thing as life not worthy to be lived. . . .
>
> [Before Hitler came to power in 1933] a propaganda barrage was directed against the traditional, compassionate, nineteenth-century attitudes towards the chronically ill, and for the adoption of a utilitarian, Hegelian point of view. Sterilization and euthanasia of persons with chronic mental illnesses was discussed at a meeting of Bavarian psychiatrists in 1931.[71]

Many people, including some in the medical profession, had accepted these principles before Hitler came on the scene.

Alexander says that Hitler exterminated 275,000 people "in these killing centers." Then he adds that those so killed were to be only "the entering wedge for extermination. . . . The methods used and the personnel trained in the killing centers for the chronically sick became the nucleus of much larger centers in the East, where the plan was to kill all Jews and Poles and to cut down the Russian population by 30,000,000." The first to be killed were the aged, the infirm, the senile and mentally retarded, and defective children. Eventually, as World War II approached, the doomed undesirables included epileptics, World War I amputees, children with badly modeled ears, and even bed wetters.

Physicians took part in this planning on matters of life and death to save society's money. Adults were propagandized, one outstanding example being a motion picture called *I Accuse,* which dealt with euthanasia. Commenting on this, Alexander reported:

> This film depicts the life history of a woman suffering from multiple sclerosis. In it her husband, a doctor, finally kills her to the accompaniment of soft piano music rendered by a sympathetic colleague in an adjoining room. Acceptance of this ideology was implanted even in the children. A widely-used high school mathematics text, *Mathematics in the Service of Political Education,* Second Edition 1935, Third Edition 1936 . . . includes problems stated in distorted terms of the cost of caring for and rehabilitating the chronically sick and crippled. One of the problems asked, for instance, is how many new housing units could be built and how many marriage-allowance loans could be given to newly-wed couples for the amount of money it cost the state to care for "the crippled and the insane."[72]

The second and most widely used edition of this textbook was issued in 1935, soon after Hitler came to power. Alexander continues:

> The first direct order for euthanasia was issued by Hitler on Sept. 1, 1939. . . . All state institutions were required to report on patients who had been ill for five years or more or who were unable to work, by filling out questionnaires giving name, race, marital status, nationality, next of kin, whether regularly visited and by whom, who bore the financial responsibility and so forth. The decision regarding which patients should be killed was made entirely on the basis of this brief information by expert consultants, most of whom were professors of psychiatry in the key universities. These consultants never saw the patients themselves.[73]

There was an organization specifically for the killing of children, which was known by the euphemistic name of Realm's Committee for Scientific Approach to Severe Illness Due to Heredity and Constitution. Transportation of the patients to killing centers was carried out by The Charitable Transport Company for the Sick. In addition, Alexander notes that The Charitable Foundation for Institutional Care was "in charge of collecting the cost of the killings from the relatives without, however, informing them what the charges were for; in the death certificates the cause of death was falsified."

Alexander, under the heading "The Early Change in Medical Attitudes," gives his warning. *It all started with the acceptance of the attitude that there is such a thing as a life not worthy to be lived.* That is exactly what is being accepted today in the abortion, infanticide, and euthanasia movements.

Continuing his warning, Alexander adds: "But it is important to realize that the infinitely small wedged-in lever from which all this entire trend of mind received its impetus was the attitude towards the nonrehabilitable sick."

This attitude is very much with us today. The "small wedged-in lever" is opening doors to what would have been inconceivable before.[74] Alexander is quite correct in adding: "It is therefore this subtle shift in emphasis of the physicians' attitude that one must thoroughly investigate."

In our present climate, resulting from the humanistic base of society (with its attitude of all things being relative), it is instructive to consider how some of today's university students in the United States regard those days of Nazi rule. Dr. Richard M. Hunt, associate dean of Harvard University's Graduate School of Arts and Science, says:

> I have taught courses at Harvard for many years. I used to teach these courses from a straight historical perspective. Recently, I tried a new approach and I call the course, "Moral Dilemma in a Repressive Society: Nazi Germany." Through case studies of issues and personalities I try to present the Nazi phenomenon from the inside, so to speak, from the experience and testimony of those who lived through the period as victims, victimizers, bystanders, true believers, and members of the resistance.
>
> To make a long story short, I was greatly surprised with the reaction of the students. I had asked for personal interpretations of moral relevant dilemmas. In their end-of-term papers, it was not a matter of indifference to Nazi oppressions that I found. Nobody attempted to minimize or explain away Nazi excesses.
>
> Rather what struck me most forcibly were the depressing fatalistic conclusions about major moral dilemmas facing the German people of that particular place and time in history.
>
> Comments like these were frequent. "And with the ever present threat of Gestapo terror, who would dare to speak out and resist? Would you? Would I? Probably not!"
>
> Most disturbing of all to me was the end of the line of such arguments. This point was reached by a few students who seemed somehow to realize the moral peril of such exculpatory judgments. Their way out was to lessen the responsibility of any individual person by dispersing the guilt among all.

Clearly some trends of our times seemed to be running towards a no-fault, that is, a guilt-free society. One might say the virtues of responsible choice, paying the penalty, taking the consequences, all appear at low ebb today.

Next time I teach this course, I hope to stress more strongly my own belief in the contingencies, the open-endedness of history. Somehow, I have got to convey the meaning of moral decisions and their relation to significant outcomes. Most important, I want to point out that single acts of individuals and strong stands of institutions at an early date do make a difference in the long run. I am through with teaching no-fault history.[75]

The attitudes expressed by Dr. Hunt's students become even more alarming when one stops to think that it is difficult to understand what is going on in one's own period of time with the same depth of perception that one has while looking back on history—as these students can do as they study Nazi Germany.

The euthanasia movement—that term is used in the broadest possible sense—is with us today in great strength and with great persuasive power. Many well-meaning people are attracted to what might seem to be the beneficial aspects of some sort of euthanasia program, because they think they can be free of the guilt of responsibility. Yet undoubtedly many have not thought about where this may lead us.

Do not dismiss contemptuously our concern about the wedge principle. When the camel gets his nose in the tent, he *will* soon be in bed with you! Historians and jurists are well aware of what we say. The first step is followed by the second. It is easy to see that if the first step is immoral, whatever follows it must be immoral. But even if the first step is moral, it does not necessarily follow that the second step will also be moral. We have to be consciously aware with each step as to what the next step is *likely* to be.

Semantic legerdemain can prepare us for accepting a horror. When the World Conference on Population Control in 1974 can refer to abortion as "a retrospective method of fertility control," we know that the euphemisms for infanticide and euthanasia can be many indeed![76] In England, some call starving a child with spina bifida (cleft spine) putting it on a "low calorie diet"!

Language itself is a subtle indicator and a powerful tool. Think of the deliberate changes in language that have been used to soften the stark impact of what is actually happening. Abortion is merely the "removal of fetal tissue," or "discontinuing" or "termination" of pregnancy. Childless couples are now "child free," a term that subtly establishes children as an unwanted burden. Language has power. The language we use actually forms the concepts we have and the results these concepts produce. Think of the Nazi use of the name *The Charitable Transport Company for the Sick* for the agency conveying people to the killing centers. But let us not be naive. Exactly the same language power is being used when the unborn baby is called "fetal tissue."[77]

We view what we are experiencing now as a critical situation which can accelerate month by month until the downhill momentum cannot be arrested. Times of monstrous inhumanity do not come about all at once; they are slipped into gradually. Often those who use certain emotional phrases or high-sounding moral tones about "freedom of the individual" and appeal to "rights" do not even know what they are starting. They see only some isolated condition they want to accomplish, but have not considered soberly the overall direction in which things are moving. At some later point they want to go backwards. But then it is too late. Mankind's selfishness and greed can be counted on to widen every breach, exploiting each to the fullest for selfish purposes.

Principal Concerns

Our concerns center around several aspects of this issue. First of all, we must say that we are proponents of the sanctity of human life—*all* human life—born and unborn; old and young; black, white, brown, and yellow. We fear the attitude of the medical profession in sanctioning abortion and in moving inexorably down the road from abortion to infanticide and finally further on to what might be unthinkable today but acceptable in a very few years—such as a widespread euthanasia program.

We are concerned that there is not more protest, outcry, or activism in regard to these issues of life and death. We can even recognize that there are people who are led to starve children to death, because they think they are doing something helpful for society. Lacking an absolute ethical standard, they have only the concept of what they think is beneficial for society to guide them. But we cannot understand why other people, those with a moral base—and we know there are many of them—do not cry out. We are concerned about this because, when the first German aged, infirm, and retarded were killed in gas chambers, there was likewise no perceptible outcry from the medical profession or from an apathetic population. It was not far from there to Auschwitz.

Surely those who call themselves Christians, having a moral base, should make these things a principal issue and be willing, even at the risk of personal sacrifice, to strive privately and publicly for the dignity and sanctity of the individual.

Although at the moment the discussion is being conducted chiefly in terms of morals and ethics, another of our concerns is: What is going to happen with the addition of the economic factor? If you are a social burden *and* an economic burden, no matter how precious life might be to you, there will be little chance of your surviving.

Let it never be said by historians in the latter days of this century that—after the Supreme Court decided on abortion in 1973 and the practice of infanticide began—there was no outcry from the medical profession and no outcry from many outside this profession. Let it never be said that the extermination program for various categories of our citizens could never have come about if the physicians of this country had stood for the moral integrity that recognizes the worth of every human life. And above everything else, let it never be said that there was no outcry from the Christians! All Christians know why people are different and have value as unique individuals—sick or well, young or old. People are unique because they are made in the image of God.

What *has* happened to the human race? Why are we afraid of being people, of being human? Of enjoying the greatest blessings that life can bring—being alive and being people of love, tenderness, gentleness, care, and concern?

It is vital that we put first *not* economics or efficiency charts and plans, but being *people*—real flesh-and-blood people. We are not to be materialistic robots who think and act like machines and will even kill to maintain their life-styles. This attitude is as stupid as it is wrong. It is stupid because such people have traded in their beautiful humanity for sawdust and ashes—for broken homes, for abortions, for starved children, and for old people locked away and even destroyed. Being a person has infinitely greater rewards for those who will consciously concentrate on being people— warm and loving people—rather than on their personal peace and affluence.

We challenge you to be a person in this impersonal age. Be human in this inhuman age. Put the people in your life first— whether perfect or marred. This is your once-in-a-lifetime chance of being "people with people." Come to your senses. You and those around you *are* people, made in the image of the personal God who created all people in His image.

We have seen how a people's world-view affects how its individuals look at themselves and others. Your basic world-view matters. It will have enormous results. A mild revulsion at people's inhumanity to one another will not change anything. Outward actions against such horrors must begin with the inward action of each individual's evaluating the basis for his standards and then assessing the application of those standards to the world around him.

In Old Testament days, God expressed special abhorrence for the Canaanite practice of infant sacrifice. With heathenism, this was not confined to the Canaanites. For example, the ancient Europeans also offered up their offspring to the gods. These people killed their offspring *in order to purchase from the gods, they hoped, their own personal peace and affluence.*

Today, indiscriminate abortion, infanticide, and euthanasia are also performed *for the personal peace and affluence of individuals.* People who destroy their own children and others', so that they can maintain their life-styles, are also sacrificing to the gods—the gods of a materialistic world-view and practice, and the god of the "self" as the egotistic center and measure of all things.

In Nazi-occupied Holland, the Dutch people often distinguished themselves by the great personal sacrifices they made in defending, hiding, protecting, and *protesting for* their fellow citizens who were Jewish. Given a decree by the Nazis that they were to perform for Hitler as the German medical profession had done, Dutch physicians refused. As a result, the Dutch medical profession has no blot on its record of performance as physician-stewards. What would have happened if the *German* physicians had refused?

A resistance leaflet circulated by the Dutch underground at that time exhorted:

> Protest against the detestable persecution of Jews!!! Organize self-defense in the factories and districts!!! Solidarity with the hard-hit Jewish section of the working people!!!
> Snatch the Jewish children from Nazi violence—take them into your family!!!
> Strike!!! Strike!!! Strike!!!
> Solidarity!!! Courage!!!
> Fight proudly for the liberation of our country!!!

The Dutch resistance movement, armed only with great courage and a few typewriters, stood against the evil of its day. Let those of us who share a high view of people use wisely these days when we have influence and the freedom to strike a great blow for the humanity, dignity, and sanctity of individuals.

Alternatives

Christians and others who wish to see an end to inhumanities, in compassion and love must offer alternative solutions to the problems. What we are about to suggest does not by any means exhaust the inventory of practical proposals we must put forward—and for which we must sacrifice our own personal peace and affluence. Such a list would be impossible to complete, so we will just give examples.

Churches and other groups opposed to abortion must be prepared to extend practical help to both the unmarried woman who is pregnant and the married woman who may be faced with the question of abortion. Merely to say to either one, "You must not have an abortion"—without being ready to involve ourselves in the problem—is another way of being inhuman.

The unmarried woman may need a place to stay. Time should be taken to tell her about the many couples who cannot have babies and who long to have a child to adopt. She will certainly need counsel about how to care for her child if she decides to keep the baby. Pleasant institutions should be available for unmarried women awaiting the birth of a baby, but each person who does not believe that abortion is right should personally be prepared to offer hospitality, financial aid, or other assistance.

Have you ever welcomed an unwed mother in your home for the months before her baby was born? Are there babies now growing happily in homes that adopted them, or living with their mothers who have a changed outlook on life and death because of the months spent in your home? Hospitality, for a great number of us, should include some period of time in our lives when we care for a pregnant woman in her waiting months.

L'Abri has become known as an example of Christians practicing community over a wide spectrum of life—intellectually and practically. In its twenty-seven-year history, there has been a succession of unwed mothers cared for, encouraged, and helped in a variety of ways. Because it has been a part of L'Abri life to make people in need a part of the family, there has been participation in some eager moments at the hospital, when a new baby is welcomed into the world as a wanted human being. L'Abri is not a "work for unwed mothers," but in all its branches a community of open homes—limited, of course, in space and in the possibility of giving personal attention. Yet L'Abri workers have been able to help a number of women who have chosen not to abort their babies.

For married women facing the problems that prompt them to consider abortion, support from a church can be a critical factor. If a mother must work, why shouldn't the church provide for her child's care? Surely such an arrangement could be worked out as an expression of the community which the church is supposed to be. The church might provide a child-care center on its own premises (too many of our churches are only one-purpose buildings) or church members might take a child into their own families for a certain number of hours each week.

We are not trying to propose a universal formula, but to emphasize that saying that abortion is wrong immediately confronts us with a challenge to be willing to share in the consequences which our advice brings. For Christians who adhere to the truth of the Bible, the importance of doing what it teaches is imperative. We are to be compassionate about people's physical needs.

The same principle can be applied to infanticide. If a family resists letting a handicapped child die after birth, the church cannot just walk away from the family or the child. From the earliest days of the church, a part of its life and testimony has always been that its members care for one another in material ways as well as otherwise. Many of the best "homes for the handicapped" had Christian beginnings. But we should also consider the practical possibility of our church's setting up a plan (to be overseen by some loving person) which schedules different church members to help in the home of a handicapped person for definite periods during the week, sharing in the hard work of this type of care.

In one of the churches Francis Schaeffer pastored in the United States, there were a mongoloid child and a mentally retarded youngster. The parents, far from wealthy, had no hope of providing special education for their children. Public services were poor. He began to spend a certain number of hours each week with the two children together. The leap forward in their achievements was a thing of joy for the whole congregation. In all his Christian work, Francis Schaeffer has never had a more satisfying ministry.

Similarly, C. Everett Koop has placed many pregnant girls with Christian families in Pennsylvania. During this sheltering, ruptured father-daughter relationships have been healed, girls have become Christians, and unwanted babies have eventually brought joy to childless couples.

Again, we are offering no universal formula. The concept of being involved in hard situations and the practical outworking of that concept are the important things. It takes effort, concern, work, and often money. Christian love and humanness mean not only saying, "Infanticide is wrong." They also mean giving part of our own personal peace and affluence to share in the results that morally correct decisions produce. That means not allowing the state to take all the responsibility. As Christians, we cannot slough off the whole burden on the state. In many cases, this means finding ourselves caring for handicapped people within the totality of the Christian community. Those in groups which are not Christian must likewise find ways of being human in the years following the birth of a handicapped child.

It is worth digressing here to insist that the positive aspects of the women's rights movement can be achieved without including abortion on the agenda. The linking of the women's movement with abortion is a deliberate strategem used by some to make this practice acceptable. This uses the women's rights movement as a vehicle to which abortion has no intrinsic relationship. Unhappily, at times the leadership of this movement has built an antihuman stance into its platform in regard to abortion-on-demand. This is hardly liberation, since—carried to its logical extreme—this arbitrary and inhuman stance can only lead to a further enslavement of women and of everyone else as well. Women cannot "liberate" themselves by aborting their babies or killing their infants. The rights of women are fundamentally rooted in the biblical view of the value of each individual human being and the sacredness of human life.

Moral obligations fall to those who stand by the principle that there is no such thing as a life not worthy to be lived. We also have a responsibility toward people with terminal illnesses and toward the dying aged. Saint Joseph's Hospice in London and The Hospice Home Care Team of New Haven, Connecticut (both institutions that had Christian beginnings) can show us some ways of dying that can affirm and enhance life. We do not know the New Haven work personally, but are familiar with a representative hospice through a friend who spent a certain number of hours there each week—reading, talking, speaking of Christian beliefs, and just *being* with the dying patients. At most such hospices, three things are done. First, all possible medical knowledge is employed to keep pain under control. Second, patients are visited, read to, and kept in almost constant contact with a loving human being, so that they are not alone and deserted in that time when, of all times, being human means not being deserted. Third, families are treated as units; the family and its needs and the individual in his need are kept together as a human unit. These hospices are not in the business of dying, but of *living* right up to the end. Is this not the natural and rightful outflow of what we Christians believe about the abnormality of death and about the future resurrection victory we will experience through Christ?

If we oppose euthanasia, we must also share the weight of caring for lonely or incapacitated older people who are not terminally ill. One of us has personal knowledge about sharing such a burden. Francis Schaeffer's mother lived in his home in Switzerland for the last seven years of her life. At first she could come down to meals, go out for rides in the mountains, attend church, and so on. Gradually this changed, and she needed constant care, especially after breaking her hip. All this was taking place in the midst of the pressures at L'Abri. Students and others took turns playing checkers with her, reading to her, talking with her, and just being with her. The family could not have done this alone—it would have been a crushing strain upon them as well as upon the work. But in the united community, not only was she well cared for, but the caring was a thing of beauty. We are sure that some of those who gave of themselves in this way are still seeing their lives enhanced by this experience, as they are scattered over the face of the earth.

Our concern is more than *not killing* the elderly and the ill. *It is giving them real life.* Of course, there must be some facilities that care for the terminally ill. In fact, Christians and others should see to it that places like St. Joseph's become models for many more such hospices. But, as long as possible and in spite of smaller apartments and the antifamily influences of our age, the old, infirm, and dying should be given the chance to be really alive in the midst of the whole spectrum of life. This includes being in relationship with the family and sharing in a Christian community. Christian doctors and others of the medical profession who stand for human life can make a special contribution in this whole area, but it is not their responsibility alone (and certainly not the responsibility of the state alone). It becomes *our* responsibility when we quite properly say, "Euthanasia is wrong."

We must be realistic. The alternatives we have discussed will demand a high price. They will cost each of us some of our personal peace and affluence. But we must do them—first of all, because they are right. This is taught in the whole of the Bible and especially in the teachings of Christ. And, second, it will be a sharing of the burdens of life, and one day it will be *our* turn to be helped—and we will be glad when we are.

The question is not the worth of the imperfect infant, the retarded child, the defective adult, and the aging individual with physical and mental signs of the aging process. The question is this: Are we worthy enough to extend ourselves to meet their needs?

If we in the second half of the twentieth century wish to be remembered well, we need to do something to stop all the evils we have been speaking about. If we sit back and do nothing, our mere passivity and apathy will lead to actively evil results by removing resistance to those who *are* active and nonapathetic. That so many are doing so little should encourage more than a mild commitment to some vague idea of doing the "right" thing, as opposed to the "wrong" thing. As people, we are only as good as our deep inner principles; we are only as good as our world-view.

In the chapters that follow, we will examine what to us is the ultimate basis for life, ethics, and an active moral stand against evil. We will look at biblical Christianity and the Bible itself. For, without a firm set of principles, without a firm world-view, there cannot and will not be any firm and continued resistance to evil— or even any cohesive unity to our own lives and private moral decisions.

CHAPTER FOUR

The Basis for Human Dignity

So far in this book we have been considering an evil as great as any
practiced in human history. Our society has put to death its own
offspring, millions upon millions of them. Our society has justified taking their lives, even claiming it a virtue to do so. It has
been said this is a new step in our progress toward a liberated
humanity.

Such a situation has not come out of a vacuum. Each of us has
an overall way of looking at the world, which influences what we
do day by day. This is what we call a "world-view." And all of us
have a world-view, whether we realize it or not. We act in accordance with our world-view, and our world-view rests on what to
us is the ultimate truth.

Materialistic Humanism: The World-View of Our Era
What has produced the inhumanity we have been considering in
the previous chapters is that society in the West has adopted a
world-view which says that all reality is made up only of matter.
This view is sometimes referred to as philosophic materialism,
because it holds that only *matter* exists; sometimes it is called
naturalism, because it says that no supernatural exists. Humanism

which begins from man alone and makes man the measure of all things usually is materialistic in its philosophy. Whatever the label, this is the underlying world-view of our society today. In this view the universe did not get here because it was created by a "supernatural" God. Rather, the universe has existed forever in some form, and its present form just happened as a result of chance events way back in time.

Society in the West has largely rested on the base that God exists and that the Bible is true. In all sorts of ways this view affected the society. The materialistic or naturalistic or humanistic world-view almost always takes a superior attitude toward Christianity. Those who hold such a view have argued that Christianity is unscientific, that it cannot be proved, that it belongs simply to the realm of "faith." Christianity, they say, rests only on faith, while humanism rests on facts.

Professor Edmund R. Leach of Cambridge University expressed this view clearly:

> Our idea of God is a product of history. What I now believe about the supernatural is derived from what I was taught by my parents, and what they taught me was derived from what they were taught, and so on. But such beliefs are justified by faith alone, never by reason, and the true believer is expected to go on reaffirming his faith in the same verbal formula even if the passage of history and the growth of scientific knowledge should have turned the words into plain nonsense.[78]

So some humanists act as if they have a great advantage over Christians. They act as if the advance of science and technology and a better understanding of history (through such concepts as the evolutionary theory) have all made the idea of God and Creation quite ridiculous.

This superior attitude, however, is strange because one of the most striking developments in the last half-century is the growth of a profound pessimism among both well-educated and less-educated people. The thinkers in our society have been admitting for a long time that they have no final answers at all.

Take Woody Allen, for example. Most people know him as a comedian, but he has thought through where mankind stands after the "religious answers" have been abandoned. In an article in *Esquire* (May 1977), he says that man is left with:

> . . . alienation, loneliness [and] emptiness verging on madness. . . .
> The fundamental thing behind *all* motivation and *all* activity is the

constant struggle against annihilation and against death. It's absolutely stupefying in its terror, and it renders anyone's accomplishments meaningless. As Camus wrote, it's not only that *he* (the individual) dies, or that *man* (as a whole) dies, but that you struggle to do a work of art that will last and then you realize that *the universe itself* is not going to exist after a period of time. Until those issues are resolved within each person—religiously or psychologically or existentially— the social and political issues will never be resolved, except in a slap-dash way.

Allen sums up his view in his film *Annie Hall* with these words: "Life is divided into the horrible and the miserable."

Many would like to dismiss this sort of statement as coming from one who is merely a pessimist by temperament, one who sees life without the benefit of a sense of humor. Woody Allen does not allow us that luxury. He speaks as a human being who has simply looked life in the face and has the courage to say what he sees. If there is no personal God, nothing beyond what our eyes can see and our hands can touch, then Woody Allen is right: life is both meaningless and terrifying. As the famous artist Paul Gauguin wrote on his last painting shortly before he tried to commit suicide: "Whence come we? What are we? Whither do we go?" The answers are *nowhere, nothing,* and *nowhere.* The humanist H. J. Blackham has expressed this with a dramatic illustration:

> On humanist assumptions, life leads to nothing, and every pretense that it does not is a deceit. If there is a bridge over a gorge which spans only half the distance and ends in mid-air, and if the bridge is crowded with human beings pressing on, one after the other they fall into the abyss. The bridge leads nowhere, and those who are pressing forward to cross it are going nowhere. . . . It does not matter where they think they are going, what preparations for the journey they may have made, how much they may be enjoying it all. The objection merely points out objectively that such a situation is a model of futility.[79]

One does not have to be highly educated to understand this. It follows directly from the starting point of the humanists' position, namely, that everything is just matter. That is, that which has existed forever and ever is only some form of matter or energy, and everything in our world now is this and only this in a more or less complex form. Thus, Jacob Bronowski says in *The Identity of Man* (1965): "Man is a part of nature, in the same sense that a stone is, or a cactus, or a camel." In this view, men and women are by chance more complex, but not unique.

Within this world-view there is no room for believing that a human being has any final distinct value above that of an animal or of nonliving matter. People are merely a different arrangement of molecules. There are two points, therefore, that need to be made about the humanist world-view. First, the superior attitude toward Christianity—as if Christianity had all the problems and humanism had all the answers—is quite unjustified. The humanists of the Enlightenment two centuries ago *thought* they were going to find all the answers, but as time has passed, this optimistic hope has been proven wrong. It is their own descendants, those who share their materialistic world-view, who have been saying louder and louder as the years have passed, "There are no final answers."

Second, this humanist world-view has also brought us to the present devaluation of human life—not technology and not overcrowding, although these have played a part. And this same world-view has given us no limits to prevent us from sliding into an even worse devaluation of human life in the future.

So it is naive and irresponsible to imagine that this world-view will *reverse* the direction in the future. A well-meaning commitment to "do what is right" will not be sufficient. Without a firm set of principles that flows out of a world-view that gives an adequate reason for a unique value to all human life, there cannot be and will not be any substantial resistance to the present evil brought on by the low view of human life we have been considering in previous chapters. It was the materialistic world-view that brought in the inhumanity; it must be a different world-view that drives it out.

An emotional uneasiness about abortion, infanticide, euthanasia, and the abuse of genetic knowledge is not enough. To stand against the present devaluation of human life, a significant percentage of people within our society must adopt and live by a world-view which not only hopes or intends to give a basis for human dignity but which really does. The radical movements of the sixties were right to hope for a better world; they were right to protest against the shallowness and falseness of our plastic society. But their radicalness lasted only during the life span of the adolescence of their members. Although these movements claimed to be radical, they lacked a sufficient root. Their world-view was incapable of giving life to the aspirations of its adherents. Why? Because it, too—like the society they were condemning—had no sufficient base. So protests are not enough. Having the right ideals is not enough. Even those with a very short memory, those who can look back only to the sixties, can see that there must be more than that. A truly radical alternative has to be found.

But where? And how?

The Search for an Adequate World-View: A Question of Method
Before we consider various possibilities, we must settle the question of method. What is it we are expecting our "answer" to answer?

There are a number of things we could consider, but at this point we want to concentrate on just two. The first is what we will call "the universe and its form," and the second is "the mannishness of man." The first draws attention to the fact that the universe around us is like an amazing jigsaw puzzle. We see many details, and we want to know how they fit together. That is what science is all about. Scientists look at the details and try to find out how they all cohere. So the first question that has to be answered is: how did the universe get this way? How did it get this *form*, this pattern, this jigsawlike quality it now has?

Second, "the mannishness of man" draws attention to the fact that human beings are different from all other things in the world. Think, for example, of creativity. People in all cultures of all ages have created many kinds of things, from "High Art" to flower arrangements, from silver ornaments to high-technology supersonic aircraft. This is in contrast to the animals about us. People also fear death, and they have the aspiration to truly choose. Incidentally, even those who in their writings say we only *think* we choose quickly fall into words and phrases that only make sense if they are wrong and we do truly choose. Human beings are also unique in that they verbalize. That is, people put concrete and abstract concepts into words which communicate these concepts to other people. People also have an inner life of the mind; they remember the past and make projections into the future. One could name other factors, but these are enough to differentiate people from the other things in the world.

What world-view adequately explains the remarkable phenomenon of the distinctiveness of human beings? There is one world-view which can explain the existence of the universe, its form, and the uniqueness of people—the world-view given to us in the Bible. There is a remarkable parallel between the way scientists go about checking to see if what they think about reality does in fact correspond to it and the way the biblical world-view can be checked to see if it is true.

Many people, however, react strongly against this sort of claim. They see the problem—Where has everything come from and why is it the way it is?—but they do not want to consider a solution which involves God. God, they say, belongs to "religion," and religious answers, they say, do not deal with facts. Only science deals with facts. Thus, they say, Christian answers are not real answers; they are "faith answers."

This is a strange reaction, because modern people pride themselves on being open to new ideas, on being willing to consider opinions which contradict what has been believed for a long time. They think this is what "being scientific" necessitates. Suddenly, however, when one crosses into the area of the "big" and most basic questions (like those we are considering now) with an answer involving God, the shutters are pulled down, the open mind closes and a very different attitude, a dogmatic *rationalism,* takes over.[80]

This is curious—first, because few seem to notice that the humanist explanation of the big and most basic questions is just as much a "faith answer" as any could be. With the humanist world-view everything begins with only matter; whatever has developed has developed only within matter, a reordering of matter by chance.

Even though materialistic scientists have no scientific understanding of *why* things exist, nor any certain scientific understanding of *how* life began, and even though this world-view leaves them with vast problems—the problems Woody Allen has described of "alienation, loneliness [and] emptiness verging on madness"—many modern people still reject at once any solution which uses the word *God,* in favor of the materialistic humanist "answer" which answers nothing. This is simply prejudice at work.

We need to understand, however, that this prejudice is both recent and arbitrary. Professor Ernest Becker, who taught at the University of California at Berkeley and San Francisco State College, said that for the last half-million years people have always believed in two worlds—one that was visible and one that was invisible. The visible world was where they lived their everyday lives; the invisible world was more powerful, for the meaning and existence of the visible world was dependent on it. Suddenly in the last century and a half, as the ideas of the Enlightenment have spread to the whole of Western culture, we have been told quite arbitrarily that there *is* no invisible world. This has become dogma for many secular people today.

Christians try to answer prejudices like these by pointing out that the biblical system does not have to be accepted blindly, any more than the scientific hypotheses have to be accepted blindly. What a scientist does is to examine certain phenomena in the world. He then casts about for an explanation that will make sense of these phenomena. That is the hypothesis. But the hypothesis has to be checked. So a careful checking operation is set up, designed to see if there is, in fact, a correspondence between what has been observed and what has been hypothesized. If it does correspond, a scientist accepts the explanation as correct; if it does not, he rejects it as false and looks for an alternative explanation. Depending on how substantially the statement has been "verified," it becomes accepted as a "law" within science, such as the law of gravity or the second law of thermodynamics.

What we should notice is the method. It is rather like trying to find the right key to fit a particular lock. We try the first key and then the next and the next until finally, if we are fortunate, one of them fits. The same principle applies, so Christians maintain, when we consider the big questions. Here are the phenomena. What key unlocks their meaning? What explanation is correct?

We may consider the materialistic humanist alternative, the Eastern religious alternative, and so on. But each of these leaves at least a part of these most basic questions unanswered. So we turn to examine the Christian alternative.

Obviously, Christians do not look on the Bible as simply an alternative. As Christians we consider it to be objectively true, because we have found that it does give the answers both in knowledge and in life. For the purposes of discussion, however, we invite non-Christians to consider it as *an* alternative—not to be accepted blindly, but for good and sufficient reasons.

But note this—the physical scientist does something very easy, compared to those who tackle the really important and central questions for mankind. He examines a tiny portion of the real world—a leaf, a cell, an atom, a particle—and, because these things are not personal and obey very precise laws, he is able to arrive at explanations with relative ease. C. F. A. Pantin, who was professor of zoology at Cambridge University, once said: "Very clever men are answering the relatively easy questions of the natural examination paper." This is not to disparage physical science. It works consistently with its own principles of investigation, looking further and further into the material of the world around us. But it only looks at part of the world. As Professor W. H. Thorpe of Cambridge University says, it is "a deliberate restriction to certain areas of our total experience—a technique for understanding certain parts of that experience and achieving mastery over nature."

We are not then moving from definite things to indefinite things, when we look at those aspects of our experience which are more central than the study of an individual physical thing such as a leaf, a cell, an atom, or a particle. Rather, we are turning from a small part of reality to a larger part of reality. Picture a scientist for a moment: he is looking at a particular detail and carrying out his scientific investigation according to the recognized procedures. We have already discussed the method he uses to find the answers. Now we need to draw back and consider the whole phenomenon we are looking at, that is, the scientist carrying out his experiment. When the scientist is seated at his desk, he is able to find answers to his questions only *because* he has made two colossal assumptions about his situation, in fact about the entire world. He is assuming first of all that the things he is looking at do fit together somehow, even if some areas—such as particle physics—cannot at this time be fitted into a simple explanation. If the scientist did not assume that the things he is studying somehow fit together, he would not be trying to find an answer. Second, he is assuming that he as a person is able to find answers.

In other words, the *big* questions constitute the very framework within which the scientist is operating. To quote Thorpe again, "I recently heard one of the most distinguished theoretical scientists state that his own scientific drive was based on two fundamental attitudes: a conviction of his own responsibility and an awe at the beauty and harmony of nature." So we have to resist any suggestion that to be involved in answering the big questions is somehow to be getting further and further away from "the real world."

The opposite is the case. It is as we come to these big questions that we approach the real world that every one of us is living in twenty-four hours a day—the world of real persons who can think and so work out problems such as how to get to the other side of town, persons who can love, persons who can make moral decisions. These are, in other words, the phenomena which cry out for an adequate explanation. These are the things we know best about ourselves and the world around us. What world-view can encompass them?

C. S. Lewis pointed out that there are only two alternatives to the Christian answer—the humanist philosophy of the West and the pantheist philosophy of the East. We would agree. We agree, too, with his observation that Eastern philosophy is an "opposite" answer to the Christian system, but we shall look at that later. For the present our attention is directed toward the materialistic world-view of the West.

From time to time we read in the press or hear on the radio that an oil tanker has run aground on rocks and that the crude oil is being driven by the wind and currents onto an otherwise beautiful coast. We can picture the problem of humanism in that way. There is a rock on which all humanist philosophy must run aground. It is the problem of relative knowledge and relative morality or, to put it another way, the problem of finiteness or limitation. Even if mankind now had perfect moral integrity regarding the world, people would still be finite. People are limited. This fact, coupled with the rejection of the possibility of having answers from God, leads humanists into the problem of relative knowledge. There *has* been no alternative to this relativity for the past 200 years, and there can be no alternative within the humanist world-view. That is what we want to show now.

How Do We Know We Know?

During the early stages of modern philosophy (as distinguished from medieval philosophy)—that is, around the seventeenth century in Europe—the question that was troubling philosophers was this: *how do we know that we know?*

The early modern scientists had made advances in the physical sciences by rejecting previous human authority. For example, they rejected much of what had been inherited from the science of the Middle Ages. At that time, investigation had been governed and restrained by the concepts of Aristotle. In the field of astronomy, this had meant that the Ptolemaic system held sway. Suddenly, observations were made which cast doubt on that entire system of understanding the heavenly bodies. The result was, of course, the Copernician revolution: the discovery that the sun does not move around the earth but, rather, the earth around the sun. Thus, a general attitude was developed toward the ideas which had prevailed till then. The scientists said, "We must not accept the ideas passed down to us or derived from various previous authorities. We must start from scratch and simply observe the world and see how it works. Otherwise, we may be hampered from seeing what is there."

The early modern scientists did not, however, reject the knowledge that God gave in the Bible as they rejected previous human authority and opinion. For example, in *Novum Organum* (1620) Francis Bacon wrote: "To conclude, therefore, let no man out of weak conceit of sobriety, or an ill applied moderation, think or maintain that a man can search too far or be too well studied in the book of God's word, or in the book of God's works."[81] "The book of God's word" is the Bible. "The book of God's works" is the world which God has made.

Modern scientists in general lived, thought, and worked in the framework of rejecting human authority, while respecting what was taught in the Bible in regard to the cosmos—right up to the time of Michael Faraday and James Clerk Maxwell in the second half of the nineteenth century.

The *philosophers* (and later the materialistic scientists) went further. Their error was to confuse the escape from past human authority (which was indeed confining) with putting man at the center and rejecting God's authority as well. They wanted to reject all outside authority. They wanted to establish everything only on human observation. That was how the question of epistemology (how we know we know) became so important in modern philosophy. It has remained so right up to our own day.

The philosopher who first raised these questions was René Descartes (1596-1650). Descartes wrote in *Meditations on First Philosophy*:

> How often it happened to me that in the night I dreamt that I found myself on this particular place . . . whilst in reality I was lying on my bed! At this moment it does seem that it is with eyes awake that I am looking at this paper. . . . But in thinking over this I remind myself that on many occasions I have in sleep been deceived by similar illusions, and in dwelling carefully on this reflection I see so manifestly that there are no certain indications by which we may clearly distinguish wakefulness from sleep that I am lost in astonishment. And my astonishment is such that it is almost capable of persuading me that I now dream.[82]

Here is the modern epistemological problem expressed three centuries ago! All knowledge comes through the senses, but how can we rely on our own senses? Sometimes, as in dreaming, we seem to be experiencing things very really, yet the reality is only in our heads.

We are reminded of the 1966 film by Michelangelo Antonioni called *Blow-Up*, in which one of the central issues was this same question. A photographer had taken a picture of a murdered man in a park in London and then became uncertain whether this was, in fact, part of reality or an experience of fantasy similar to a drug trip. Within the humanist world-view there is no final way of telling. And Antonioni ends his film by making the point graphically. Tennis players play the game without a ball. The invisible "ball" goes back and forth and the spectators watch its "path" from side to side until finally the "ball" (which does not exist) goes out over the surrounding wire and "falls" at the photographer's feet. He pauses for a moment, uncertain about what he should do. (Is observation simply a matter of the majority? Does the reality of things come from the general agreement in society and nothing more?) Then the photographer stoops down, picks up the "ball," and throws it back onto the court. Here, depicted brilliantly, is the problem of any system which builds its epistemology on man alone. This film was a philosophic statement of the period in which we are living.

Take another example out of the history of this new approach in philosophy, that of David Hume (1711-1776). In 1732 he shocked the world with *A Treatise of Human Nature*. John Locke (1632-1704) had already denied the concept of "innate ideas" of right and wrong; that is, Locke denied that these ideas are inherent in the mind from birth. This had troubled many. Then Hume burst on the scene with a challenge which went further.

What was most startling was his progression beyond skepticism concerning God and other things of the "invisible world" to a skepticism about the visible world as well. Among other things, he questioned the concept of causality. That is, Hume challenged the notion that there is a reality in the external world which leads us to speak about one thing as being the cause of another. When we see a tree bending and swaying and its leaves falling to the ground and racing off across the field, we naturally speak of the wind as *causing* this phenomenon. Hume challenged this.

Following on from Locke, who said that all knowledge comes only from the senses, Hume argued that causality is *not* perceived by the senses. What we *perceive* are two events following closely upon each other. It was custom, he argued, which led us to speak in terms of causality, not any objective "force" working in the things themselves. Anyone can see where this thinking leads, and it was so understood at the time. If causality is not real, science becomes impossible—for what scientists are doing is tracing the path of cause and effect from one event to the next.

A modern British humanist, Kathleen Nott, has written perceptively about Hume in *Objections to Humanism* (1967): "Among great philosophers, Hume . . . hung his nose as far as any over the nihilistic abyss."[83] This is right. Hume was questioning the most basic elements of our experience. Yet he was trying to be consistent to his presuppositions (that is, his starting point). Where did this lead him? To a skepticism about knowledge itself. Hume wrote designedly against the Christian world-view which prevailed in England at the time. He wanted to dismantle the system of ideas which came out of the Bible, of a God before whom man was responsible, of people being more than matter, of a life after death which seemed to defy all natural law. Where he ended, though, was with uncertainty even about the ordinary things of life. As Kathleen Nott continues: "Hume's philosophizing was indeed a radical skepticism, which left no convincing logical grounds for believing that anything natural, let alone supernatural, was there at all."[84]

But there is something even more striking about Hume. Skepticism was the direction in which his philosophy led him; yet he was not able to live with it himself. He "hung his nose over the nihilistic abyss"—and we can picture him standing on the edge and peering over—but what then? Nott says he "withdrew it sharply when he saw the psychological risks involved." Hume himself said in *A Treatise of Human Nature* (Volume I):

Should it be asked me whether I sincerely assent to this argument which I have been to such pains to inculcate, and whether I be really one of those skeptics who hold that all is uncertain . . . I . . . should reply . . . that neither I nor any other person was ever sincerely and constantly of that opinion. . . . I dine, I play backgammon, I converse and am merry with my friends; and when, after 3 or 4 hours amusement, I would return to these speculations, they appear so cold and strained and ridiculous that I cannot find in my heart to enter into them any further. Thus the skeptic still continues to reason and believe, though he asserts that he cannot defend his reason by reason;

and by the same rule, he must assent to the principle concerning the existence of body, though he cannot pretend, by any argument of philosophy, to maintain its veracity.[85]

We believe there are only two basic alternatives in the search for the source of knowledge. One is that a person attempts to find the answers to all his questions alone. The other is that he seeks revealed truths from God. We shall come to the second later. Now we are looking at the former, and we are suggesting that this is the basic problem with which all humanistic systems must wrestle: the problem of knowledge.

We could go into many other details concerning the subsequent history of the ideas we have dealt with, including in particular Immanuel Kant (1724-1804) and his own "Copernician revolution" in philosophy and also the developments surrounding Ludwig Wittgenstein (1889-1951) and linguistic philosophy in the twentieth century. We shall stop here, partly to keep the discussion of modern philosophy from becoming too technical, but mainly because the basic difficulties had already been expressed within a century of the birth of modern philosophy.

Starting with himself, a person cannot establish an adequate explanation for the amazing possibility that he can observe the world around him and be assured that his observations have a correspondence with reality. The problem is not just that a person cannot know everything. The need is not for exhaustive knowledge; the need is for a base for any knowledge at all. That is, even though we know we cannot exhaustively perceive even the smallest things in our experience, we want assurance that we have really perceived something—that is "perception" is not simply an "image" in our brain, a model or symbol of reality which we have projected out from ourselves. We want to know that we have had a *real* contact with reality. Even Hume had to admit that his philosophizing did not make sense, that it did not fit into his own experience of the world. On the humanist side this is the great tension—to have no reason for reason and yet at the same time to have to live continuously on the reality of reason.

At this point, someone is bound to ask, "But why is it necessary to have an 'adequate explanation' for knowledge?" Agreeing that Descartes, Hume, and others could find no theoretical base which tied in with their experience, isn't it sufficient to just *reason*? Probably many of you have been wanting to ask this, as you have followed along. It is a good question, for the bulk of the world never bothers about the issues which Locke, Hume, and others like them raised. Most people simply live, going about their daily lives, never troubling themselves about reality and fantasy, the subject and the object, and so on. And we are not suggesting that their experience *in itself* is invalid, as if to imply that they are not perceiving and knowing the universe around them. They are. What we *are* saying is that—whether they know it or not—their experience is possible only because they are living in the universe the Bible describes, that is, in a universe which was created by God. Their internal faculty of knowing was made by God to correspond to the world and its form which He made and which surrounds them.

If, however, we attempt to bypass the question, "Why is it possible for man to have knowledge in this way?" we must then remember the other two great problems of any system which starts only from man. Recall the illustration of the oil tanker and the rock. The rock is the problem of knowledge which we have been considering. That is the central problem. But there are two forms of pollution which flow from the broken ship of knowledge: first, the meaninglessness of all things and, second, the relativity of morals.

The Meaninglessness of All Things

An overwhelming number of modern thinkers agree that seeing the universe and man from a humanist base leads to meaninglessness, both for the universe and for man—not just mankind in general but for each of us as individuals. Professor Steven Weinberg of Harvard University and the Smithsonian Astrophysical Observatory has written a book entitled *The First Three Minutes: A Modern View of the Origin of the Universe* (1976). Here he explains, as clearly as probably anyone has ever done, the modern materialistic view of the universe and its origin.

But when his explanation is finished and he is looking down at the earth from an airplane, as Weinberg writes, "It is very hard to realize that this all is just a tiny part of an overwhelmingly hostile universe . . . [which] has evolved from an unspeakably unfamiliar early condition, and faces a future extinction of endless cold or intolerable heat. The more the universe seems comprehensible, the more it also seems pointless."[86]

When Weinberg says that the universe seems more "comprehensible," he is, of course, referring to our greater understanding of the physical universe through the advance of science. But it is an understanding, notice, within a materialistic framework, which considers the universe solely in terms of physics and chemistry—simply machinery. Here lies the irony. It is comprehension of a sort, but it is like giving a blind person sight, only to remove anything seeable. As we heard Woody Allen saying earlier, such a view of reality is "absolutely stupefying in its terror, and it renders anyone's accomplishments meaningless."

So, to the person who wants to be left alone without explanations for the big questions, we must say very gently, "Look at what you are left alone with." This is not merely rhetoric. As the decades of this century have slipped by, more and more have said the same thing as Steven Weinberg and Woody Allen. It has become an obvious thing to say. The tremendous optimism of the nineteenth century, which stemmed from the Enlightenment of the eighteenth century, has gradually ebbed away.

If everything "faces a future extinction of endless cold or intolerable heat," all things are meaningless. This is the first problem, the first form of pollution. The second is just as bad.

The Relativity of Morals

The material universe in itself gives no basis for values. Those who begin with the material universe can *describe* but they can never *define*. They can speak only in the indicative, never in the imperative. They can describe, for example, what physical strength involves and how it works physiologically, but from the material universe alone they cannot derive any idea as to how strength *ought* and *ought not* to be used. The most they can do is argue that certain moral systems have been worked out through the passage of time on the basis of "social contact." This is what we call the 51 percent view of morality—the majority has thought such and such is a good way to operate and so it becomes "morality." What confusion! What disaster! With this view any action can be justified, and our own very recent history has given us appalling examples.

Aldous Huxley said it all clearly in the thirties in his brilliant little novel *Brave New World*. In it he pictures a society which has reversed the morality of the present, especially in the area of sexual relationships. Faithfulness within a unique love relationship becomes "evil"; promiscuity becomes "good."[87]

Here then is the humanist dilemma. They have to generate the answers to the big questions, but out of their own limited experience they can know *nothing* with certainty. If we were to add up the thinking of *all* of mankind, we would still have only limited knowledge. *Truth* with a capital *T*—explanations which would be true for all time and all people—would be impossible.

What is left, therefore, is "relative" truth, and with relative truth, relative morality. Given time, even the "certainties" of our ethical systems can be undone—the bills of rights, the charters of freedom, the principles of justice, everything. Aleksandr Solzhenitsyn understands this not only as a theoretical problem of a humanistic philosophy. He has suffered under its implications. He writes:

> Communism has never concealed the fact that it rejects all absolute concepts of morality. It scoffs at good and evil as indisputable categories. Communism considers morality to be relative. Depending upon circumstances, any act, including the killing of thousands, could be good or bad. It all depends upon class ideology, defined by a handful of people. . . . It is considered awkward to use seriously such words as good and evil. But if we are to be deprived of these concepts, what will be left? We will decline to the status of animals.

We in the West must understand that it is not only Iron Curtain countries who operate on the basis of relative morality. Now the West does, too. The materialist world-view has dominated the thinking of the West just as much. Therefore we can expect to see the same inhumanity here, just as Solzhenitsyn has warned. We must not sit back and think, *It could never happen here.* Worse still, we must not be confused into thinking the issue is principally or only military or economic power. The issue is more subtle, more immediate, a cancerlike growth which is in our midst right now— the materialist philosophy which underlies the Western humanistic world-view. Marx may have proposed an economic system different from our own, but we have shared his basic world-view.

The greatest dilemma for those who hold this world-view, however, is that it is impossible to live consistently within it. We saw how this was true of David Hume. Likewise the playwright Samuel Beckett can "say" that words do not communicate any-thing—and that everything, including language, is absurd—yet he must use words to write his plays, even plays about meaningless-ness. If the words that Beckett uses did not convey meaning to his hearers, he could not say that everything, including words, is meaningless.

The list of contradictions can be extended endlessly. The truth is that everyone who rejects the biblical world-view must live in a state of tension between ideas about reality and reality itself.

Thus, if a person believes that everything is only matter or energy and carries this through consistently, meaning dies, morality dies, love dies, hope dies. *Yet!* The individual does love, does hope, does act on the basis of right and wrong. This is what we mean when we say that everyone is caught, regardless of his world-view, simply by the way things are. No one can make his own universe to live in.

The reason for this, as we have said all along, is that the individual is confronted with two aspects of reality that do not basically change: the universe and its form and the mannishness of man. Humanists argue that everything is finally only matter or energy and end up with no answers to the big questions. They arrive at only meaninglessness, relative morality, relative knowledge. But humanists actually live as if there *is* meaning and real morality. They act, for example, as if cruelty is not the same as noncruelty, or justice the same as injustice. Also, humanists do have knowledge, knowledge of a world in which causality is real and science is possible.

Exactly the same dilemma exists with the other main alternative to Christianity: the philosophies of the East. Despite their many differences, all of these philosophies flow out of the view that ultimately everything is impersonal. The universe we are experiencing, the Eastern philosophers say, is simply an extension of God, but—and here we need to be careful—they do not mean that God is personal. "God" means the "impersonal everything," which has no final distinctions. So, within this view, the solution is to say we must get rid of those aspirations that are personal, those things that make us seem to be independent entities, entirely independent selves. Such an idea is *maya,* that is, "illusion."

In the Eastern thinking, the only reality is *one* beyond all distinctions and therefore impersonal: no "male" or "female," no "you" or "me," no "good" or "evil." It is important to note that Eastern thinkers come to exactly the same place as those who begin by saying that everything is matter or energy. At first the two positions sound very different, but they result in the same final position.

And so we ask again: Can a person espousing this Eastern world-view live consistently with it? In his 1974 book *Zen and the Art of Motorcycle Maintenance,* Robert M. Pirsig relates an interesting anecdote. The author, who calls himself Phaedrus in the story, studied philosophy at Benares University for about ten years. He tells how his time there came to an end.

> One day in the classroom the professor of philosophy was blithely expounding on the illusory nature of the world for what seemed the fiftieth time and Phaedrus raised his hand and asked coldly if it was believed that the atomic bombs that had dropped on Hiroshima and Nagasaki were illusory. The professor smiled and said yes. That was the end of the exchange.
> . . . Within the traditions of Indian philosophy that answer may have been correct, but for Phaedrus and for anyone else who reads newspapers regularly and is concerned with such things as mass destruction of human beings that answer was hopelessly inadequate. He left the classroom, left India and gave up.[88]

There are, then, only two main alternative world-views to Christianity, both of which begin with the impersonal. The West has a *materialistic* view and is nonreligious. The East has an *immaterialistic* view and is religious. *But both are impersonal systems.* This is the important point; by comparison, their differences pale into insignificance. The result is that, in both the West and the East, men and women are seen as abnormal aliens to the way things really are. In Eastern terms they are spoken of as *maya* or illusion; in Western terms, as absurd machines.

Relieving the Tension in the West
In both the East and the West, however, there are attempts to relieve the tension of seeming to be nothing, while in fact being something very real—a person in a real world which has a definite form. On the materialist side, Sir Julian Huxley (1887-1975) has clarified the dilemma by acknowledging, though he was an atheist, that somehow or other—against all that one might expect—a person functions better if he acts *as though God exists.* "So," the argument goes, "God does not in fact exist, but act as if He does!" As observed by the Norwegian playwright Henrik Ibsen (1828-1906) in *The Wild Duck:* "Rob the average man of his life-illusion, and you rob him of his happiness at the same stroke." In other words, according to Huxley, you can function properly only if you live your whole life upon a lie. You act as if God exists, which to the

materialist is false. At first this sounds like a feasible solution for relieving the tension produced by a materialistic world-view. However, a moment's reflection shows what a terrible solution it is. You will find no deeper despair than this for a sensitive person. This is no optimistic, happy, reasonable, brilliant answer. It is darkness and death.

Another way the tension is relieved is through the theory of evolution, the idea that *by chance* there is an increasing advance. People are given an impression of progress—up from the primeval slime and the amoeba, up through the evolutionary chain, with life developing by chance from the simple carbon molecule to the complex, right up to the pinnacle, mankind.

This is not the place to discuss evolutionary theory, but it surprises us how readily people accept it, even on the scientific side, as if it had no problems. There are problems, even if these are not commonly realized or discussed.[89] The primary point we are interested in, however, is not evolution itself but the illusion of "progress" which has been granted by it. By chance, this amazing complexity called "man" has been generated out of the slime. So, of course, there is progress! By this argument people are led into imagining that the whole of reality does have purpose even if, as we have said, there is no way that it really can have purpose within the humanistic world-view.

Evolution makes men and women feel superior and at the top of the pile, but in the materialistic framework, the whole of reality is meaningless; the concept of "higher" means nothing. Even if, within the humanist world-view, people are more complex than plants and animals, both "higher" and "lower" have no meanings. We are left with everything being sad and absurd.

Thus, the concept of progress is an illusion. Only some form of mystical jump will allow us to accept that personality comes from impersonality.[90] No one has offered to explain, let alone demonstrate it to be feasible, how the impersonal plus time plus chance can give personality. We are distracted by a flourish of words—and, lo, personality has appeared out of a hat.

Imagine a universe made up of only liquids and solids, one containing no free gases. A fish is swimming in this universe. This fish, quite naturally, is conformed to its environment so that it is able to exist quite happily. Let us suppose, then, that by blind chance (as the evolutionists would have us believe) this fish developed lungs as it continued swimming in this universe without any gases. This fish would no longer be able to function and to fulfill its position as a fish. Would it then be "higher" or "lower" in its new state with lungs? Obviously it would be lower, for it would drown.

In the same way, if a person has been kicked up from the impersonal by chance, those things that make him a person—hope of purpose and significance, love, notions of morality and rationality and beauty—are ultimately unfulfillable and are thus meaningless. In such a situation, is man higher or lower? Mankind would then be the lowest creature on the scale, the least conforming to what reality is. Thus we see how hopeless is the illusion of meaning or purpose as derived from evolutionary thought.

Relieving the Tension in the East
Within Eastern thinking, attempts to relieve the tension have been made by introducing "personal gods." To the uninitiated these gods seem to be real persons; they are said to appear to human beings and even have sexual intercourse with them. But they are not really personal. Behind them their souce is the "impersonal everything" of which they are simply emanations. We find a multitude of gods and goddesses with their attendant mythologies, like the *Ramayana,* which then give the simple person a "feeling" of personality in the universe. People need this, because it is hard to live as if there is nothing out there in or beyond the universe to which they can relate personally. The initiated, however, understand. They know that ultimate reality is impersonal. So they submit themselves to the various techniques of the Eastern religions to eliminate their "personness." Their goal is to achieve a state of consciousness not bounded by the body and the senses or even by such ideals as "love" or "good."

Probably the most sophisticated Eastern attempt to deal with the tension we are considering is the Bhagavad-Gita. This is a religious writing probably produced around 200 B.C. in India. It has been the inspiration for multitudes of Hindus through the centuries and most notably for Indian spiritual and political leader Mahatma Gandhi. In it the individual is urged to participate in acts of charity. At the same time, however, the individual is urged to enter into these acts in "a spirit of detachment." Why? Because the proper attitude is to understand that none of these experiences really matter. It is the state of consciousness that rises above personality which is important, for personality is, after all, an abnormality within the impersonal universe.

Alternatively, the East proposes a system of "endless cycles" to try to give some explanation tor things which exist about us. This has sometimes been likened to the ocean. The ocean casts up waves for a time, but the waves are still a part of the ocean, and then the waves pull back into the ocean and disappear. Interestingly enough, the Western materialist also tries to explain the form of the universe by a theory of endless cycles. He says that impersonal material or energy always exists, but that this goes through endless cycles, taking different forms—the latest of which began with the "big bang" which spawned the present expanding universe. Previously, billions and billions of years ago, this eternal material or energy had a different form and had contracted into the heavy mass from which came the present cycle of our universe. Both the Eastern thought and the Western put forth this unproven idea of endless cycles because their answers finally answer nothing.

We have emphasized the problems involved in these two alternatives because they are real. It is helpful to see that the only serious intellectual alternatives to the Christian position have such endless difficulties that they actually are nonanswers. We do it, too, because we find people in the West who imagine that Christianity has nothing to say on these big issues and who discard the Bible without ever considering it. This superior attitude, as we said earlier, is quite unfounded. The real situation is very different. The humanists of the Enlightenment acted as if they would conquer all before them, but two centuries have changed that.

One would have imagined at this point that Western man would have been glad for a solution to the various dilemmas facing him and would have welcomed answers to the big questions. But people are not as eager to find the truth as is sometimes made out. The history of Western thought during the past century confirms this.

Reason Is Dead
The hallmark of the Enlightenment had been "Reason Is King." The leading thinkers had consciously rejected the need for revelation. As Paul Hazard in *European Thought in the Eighteenth Century* says, they put Christianity on trial.[91]

Gradually, however, the problems of this enthronement of human reason emerged. The reason of man was not big enough to handle the big questions, and what man was left with was relative knowledge and relative morality. This noose around the humanist's neck tightened with every passing decade and generation.

What would he do?

Ironically, even though the basis of the humanists' whole endeavor had been the central importance of man's reason, when faced with the problems of relative knowledge and relative morality they repudiated reason. Rather than admit defeat in front of God's revelation, the humanists extended the revolution further—and in a direction which would have been quite unthinkable to their eighteenth-century predecessors. Modern irrationalism was born.

We could go as far back as Immanuel Kant (1724-1804) in philosophy and to Friedrich Schleiermacher (1768-1834) in theology. Modern existentialism is also related to Søren Kierkegaard (1813-1855). However, our intention here is neither to go into the history of irrationalism, nor to examine the proponents of existentialism in our own century, but rather to concentrate on its main thesis. It is this that confronts us on all sides today, and it is impossible to understand modern man without understanding this concept.

Because we shall be using several terms a great deal now, we would ask the reader to attend carefully. When we speak of *irrationalism* or *existentialism* or *the existential methodology,* we are pointing to a quite simple idea. It may have been expressed in a variety of complicated ways by philosophers, but it is not a difficult concept.

Imagine that you are at the movies watching a suspense film. As the story unfolds, the tension increases until finally the hero is trapped in some impossible situation and everyone is groaning inwardly, wondering how he is going to get out of the mess. The suspense is heightened by the knowledge (of the audience, not the hero) that help is on the way in the form of the good guys. The only question is: *will the good guys arrive in time?*

Now imagine for a moment that the audience is slipped the information that there are no good guys, that the situation of the hero is not just desperate, but completely hopeless. Obviously, the first thing that would happen is that the suspense would be gone. You and the entire audience would simply be waiting for the axe to fall.

If the hero faced the end with courage, this would be morally edifying, but the situation itself would be tragic. If, however, the hero acted *as if* help were around the corner and kept buoying himself up with this thought ("Someone is on the way!"—"Help is at hand!''), all you could feel for him would be pity. It would be a means to keep hope alive within a hopeless situation. The hero's hope would change nothing *on the outside;* it would be unable to manufacture, out of nothing, good guys coming to the rescue. All it would achieve would be the hero's own mental state of hopefulness rather than hopelessness.

The hopefulness itself would rest on a lie or an illusion and thus, viewed objectively, would be finally absurd. And if the hero really knew what the situation was, but consciously used the falsehood to buoy up his feelings and go whistling along, we would either say, "Poor guy!" or "He's a fool." It is this kind of conscious deceit that someone like Woody Allen has looked full in the face and will have none of.

Now this is what the existential methodology is about. If the universe we are living in is what the materialistic humanists say it is, then with our reason (when we stop to think about it) we could find absolutely no way to have meaning or morality or hope or beauty. This would plunge us into despair. We would have to take seriously the challenge of Albert Camus (1913-1960) in the first sentence of *The Myth of Sisyphus:* "There is but one truly serious philosophical problem, and that is suicide."[92] Why stay alive in an absurd universe? Ah! But that is *not* where we stop. We say to ourselves—"There *is* hope!" (even though there is no help). "We shall overcome!" (even though nothing is more certain than that we shall be destroyed, both individually at death and cosmically with the end of all conscious life). This is what confronts us on all sides today: the modern irrationalism.

Long Live Experience!
Another way to understand all this is to say that modern man has become a mystic. The word *mystic* makes people think immediately of a religious person—praying for hours, using techniques of meditation, and so on. Of course, the word *mysticism* includes this, but modern mysticism is different in a profound way. As the late Professor H. R. Rookmaaker of the Free University of Amsterdam said, modern mysticism is "a nihilistic mysticism, *for God is dead.*"

The mystics within the Christian tradition (Meister Eckhart in the thirteenth century, for example) believed in an objective personal God. But, they said, though God is really there, the mind is not the way to reach Him. On the other hand, modern mysticism comes from a quite different background, and this we must be clear about.

When modern philosophers realized they were not going to be able to find answers on the basis of reason, they crossed over in one way or another to the remarkable position of saying, "That doesn't matter!" Even though there are no answers by way of the mind, we will find them without the mind. The "answer"—whatever that may be—is to be "experienced," for it cannot be thought. Notice, the answer is not to be the experience of an objective and supernatural God whom, as the medieval mystics thought, it was difficult to understand with the mind. The developments we are considering came *after* Friedrich Nietzsche (1844-1900) had celebrated the "death of God," *after* the materialist philosophy had worked its way throughout the culture and created skepticism about the supernatural.

The modern mystic, therefore, is not trying to "feel" his way to a God he believes is really there (but whom he cannot approach by way of the mind). The modern mystic does not know if *anything* is there. All he knows is that he cannot know anything ultimate through the mind. So what is left is *experience as experience*. This is the key to understanding modern man in the West: Forget your mind; just experience! It may seem extreme—but we say it carefully—this is the philosophy by which the majority of people in the West are now living. For everyday purposes the mind is a useful instrument, but for the things of meaning, for the answers to the big questions, it is set aside.

"Whatever Reality may be, it is beyond the conception of the finite intellect; it follows that attempts at descriptions are misleading, unprofitable, and a waste of time." That is a quotation from a modern Buddhist in the West. The secular existentialists may seem a long way from such an Eastern formulation about reality, but their rejection of the intellect as a means of finding answers amounts to the same thing. That is what the existentialist "revolt," as it has been called, is. It is a revolt against the mind, a passionate rejection of the Enlightenment ideal of reason. As Professor William Barrett of New York University has put it: "Existentialism is the counter-Enlightenment come at last to philosophic expression."[93]

The way to handle philosophy, according to the existential methodology, is not by the use of the mind that considers (impersonally and objectively) propositions about reality. Rather, the way to deal with the big questions is by relying only on the individual's experience. That which is being considered is not necessarily an experience of something that really exists. What is involved is the experience *as an experience,* whether or not any objective reality is being experienced. We are reminded of our imaginary hero who said, "Help is coming," and therefore kept himself going, even though he had no reason to think any help existed. It is the experience as the experience that counts, and that is the end of it.

There are, of course, some valuable insights in what the existentialists have said. For one, they were right to protest against scientism and the impersonalism of much post-Enlightenment thought. They were right to point out that answers have to be "lived" and not just "thought." (We will say more about this in Chapter 6.) But their rejection of the mind is no solution to anything. It *seems* like a solution but is in fact a counsel of despair.

Having started with the apparently different positions of the Buddhist and the secular existentialist, we should now look at culture at large. One of the "cultural breakpoints" was Haight-Ashbury in the sixties. There the counterculture, the drug culture, was born. Writing about the experience of Ken Kesey and his Merry Pranksters in the early days of Haight-Ashbury, Tom Wolfe says,

> Gradually the Prankster attitude began to involve the main things religious mystics have always felt, things common to Hindus, Buddhists, Christians, and for that matter Theosophists and even flying-saucer cultists. Namely, the experiencing of an Other World, a higher level of reality. . . .
> Every vision, every insight . . . came out of the *new experience.* . . . And how to get it across to the multitudes who have never had this experience for themselves? *You couldn't put it into words.* You had to create conditions in which they would *feel* an approximation of that *feeling,* the sublime kairos (*italics* added).

Do you see what is involved here? We can agree this represents a wild-fringe element of the counterculture which is already behind us. But we must understand that the central ideas and attitudes are now part of the air we breathe in the West. "Every insight . . . came out of the new experience." *Experience!*—that is the word! And how to tell it? "You couldn't put it into words."

The New Mysticism
What about the spread of Eastern religions and techniques within the West—things like TM, Yoga, the cults? We have moved beyond the counterculture of the sixties, but where to? These elements from the East no longer influence just the beat generation and the dropouts. Now they are fashionable for the middle classes as well. They are everywhere.

What has become important is not whether there is anything that causes an experience, but just the experience as such. What about modern theology in the churches? It is the same thing. Maybe the terminology is "Christian," but the ideas are on the other side—experience is the important thing, not propositions about reality, about God, about salvation and all the rest. It does not matter if anything exists that has caused or conforms to the experience.

What about the sudden growth of interest in UFOs and UFOlogy? Even though not a scrap of evidence exists to support Erich von Däniken's "scientific" theories about spacemen who visited earth in the distant past, millions of people have been taken with these assumptions. He has given his ideas an aura of scientific plausibility, plenty of technical jargon, photographs, and so forth, and because this is a "scientific age," people are impressed. But the real evidence is unconvincing. Is there conscious life in other parts of the cosmos? We do not know. If there is, it would pose no problem for Christianity. Still, at this time there is no proof at all that this is the case. Why then do people accept it? We suggest it is part of the swing to the irrational.

People are hungry for something which will give them hope in life. They are tired of the empty platitudes that politicians and many theologians have made: endless exhortations to be good, to be good, to be good! They are also afraid. Things really do seem hopeless, even on the level of everyday life with its threats of a lower standard of living, of a growing authoritarianism, of famine and ecological disaster, of devastating war. And they are looking for *any* answer. So the UFOs are messengers of a friendly race from another planet. "Do not fear—the Force is with you!"—to borrow from a current science-fiction film. And so people believe it irrationally. If they used their minds, they would see no evidence for friendly people from outside. But the feeling of experience as they read about this or see it on a screen is enough. It does not matter whether there is any reality to it.

What about the growth of occultism, witchcraft, astrology? Is it simply economics that has put the signs of the zodiac in shops from one end of our society to the other? In part it is economics, but, once again, the real reason is deeper. People are looking for answers—answers they can experience.

What about those who take drugs as a means of "expanding their consciousness"? This, too, is in the same direction. Your mind is a hindrance to you: "Blow it"! As Timothy Leary put it in *The Politics of Ecstasy* (1968): "Our favorite concepts are standing in the way of a flood tide two billion years building up. The verbal dam is collapsing. Head for the hills or prepare your intellectual craft to flow with the current." So we see again the rejection of the mind. The verbal dam, the concepts, the intellectual craft? These must be bypassed by the "new man."

Wherever we look, this is what confronts us: irrational experience. We must be careful not to be bewildered by the surface differences between these movements. We are not saying they are all the same. Of course there are differences. The secular existentialists, for example, disagree with one another. Then, too, secular existentialists differ with religious existentialists; the former tend to be pessimistic, the latter optimistic. Some of the movements are serious and command our respect. Some are just bizarre. There *are* differences. *Yet, all of them represent the new mysticism!*

The problem with mysticism of this sort is, interestingly enough, the same problem we considered earlier in relation to all humanistic systems. Who is going to say what is right?

As soon as one removes the checking mechanism of the mind by which to measure things, everything can then be "right" and everything can also be "wrong." Eventually, anything and everything can be allowed! Take a simple example from life: If you are asking for directions in a city, you first listen to the directions your guide is giving and then you set off. Let us say the directions are: "Take the first turn on the right, called Twenty-fourth Street; then the next turn on the left, called Kennedy Drive; and then keep going till you come to the park where you will see the concert hall just past a big lake on your right." Armed with these directions, you go along—checking up on what you have been told: "Yes, there is Twenty-fourth Street. Yes, there is Kennedy Drive," and so on.

In other words, you are not just told words; you are able to see if these words relate to the outside world, the world you have to operate in if you are going to get from *A* to *B*. This is where your mind is essential. You can check to see if the information you have been given is true or false.

Imagine, on the other hand, that someone said, in answer to your request for directions, "I don't know where or what *B* is. It is impossible to talk about a 'concert hall.' What is a 'concert hall' anyway? We can only say of it that it is the 'Unknowable.' " How completely ridiculous for you to be told, "Go *any* way—because this is the way"!

The trick in all these positions is to argue first of all that the End—Final Reality—cannot be spoken of (because it cannot be known by the mind) and yet to give the directions to find it. We should notice, however, that in this setting we can never ask questions ahead of time about the directions we receive. They are directions only for blindfolded experience, the blind "leap of faith."

We cannot ask, "How will I know that it is truth or that it is the divine I am experiencing?" The answer is always, "There is no way you can be told, for it is an answer beyond language, beyond categories, but take this path [or that one, or another one] anyway."

Thus, modern man is bombarded from all sides by devotees of this or that *experience.* The media only compound the problem. So does the commercialism of our highly technological societies. The danger of manipulation from these alone is overwhelming. In the absence of a clear standard, they are a force for the control of people's minds and behavior that is beyond anything in history. In fact, there are no clear standards in Western society now; and where there is an appearance of standards, very often there is insufficient motivation to lean against the enormous pressures. And why? In part, at least, because there is an inadequate basis for knowledge and for morality.

When we add to this that modern man has become a "mystic," we soon realize the seriousness of the situation. For in all these mystical solutions no one can finally say anything about right and wrong. The East has had this problem for thousands of years. In a pantheistic system, whatever pious statements may be made along the way, ultimately good and evil are equal in God, the impersonal God. So we hear Yun-Men, a Zen master, saying, "If you want to get the plain truth, be not concerned with right and wrong. Conflict between right and wrong is the sickness of the mind."

Society can have no stability on this Eastern world-view or its present Western counterpart. It just does not work. And so one finds a gravitation toward some form of authoritarian government, an individual tyrant or group of tyrants who takes the reins of power and rule. And the freedoms, the sorts of freedoms we have enjoyed in the West, are lost.

We are, then, brought back to our starting point. The inhumanities and the growing loss of freedoms in the West are the result of a world-view which has no place for "people." Modern humanistic materialism is an impersonal system. The East is no different. Both begin and end with impersonality.

We have looked at reasons for concluding not merely that these world-views are uncomfortable because they lead to inhumanity, but because they are false. They do not fit into what we know best about ourselves and our environment. Ours is a universe which contains real personality. Neither the universe nor this personality is illusory. We will turn now to the Bible's claim to be the reliable source of information about the universe and mankind. But first, there are two very important introductory comments.

The Unveiling of Truth
The famous Hindu writer and statesman Sarvepalli Radhakrishnan once wrote, "The altars erected to the unknown gods in the Graeco-Roman world were but an expression of man's ignorance of the divine nature. The sense of failure in man's quest for the unseen is symbolized by them. When asked to define the nature of God, the seer of the Upanishad sat silent, and when pressed to answer claimed that the Absolute is silence."

By contrast, the Apostle Paul, speaking in the context of the very same altars to unknown gods in Athens, said, ". . . Now what you worship as something unknown I am going to proclaim to you" (Acts 17:23). And again, writing to the Corinthians not far away, "However, as it is written: 'No eye has seen, nor ear has heard, no mind has conceived . . .' but God has revealed it to us . . ." (1 Corinthians 2:9, 10). This claim is common to the whole Bible. God has not waited for us to stumble to Him in the dark (which would be impossible anyway), but has revealed Himself to us. The word *revelation* in Greek is *apokalupsis* which means literally "unveiling"; so God has "unveiled" to us the things we could not know because of our finiteness and sin.

This revelation or unveiling to finite and sinful people is the

Bible as the *written Word*. This is the claim of the whole Bible. Moreover, through the Bible we learn of the life and teaching of the Second Person of the Trinity, who became man at a point in history and so became the *Living Word* of the Godhead: "For in Christ all the fullness of the Deity lives in bodily form" (Colossians 2:9).

In this claim the dilemma of all humanistic systems is overcome at a stroke. The *infinite* God has spoken. None of the many finite attempts to define truth, doomed to failure as we have seen, is necessary. God has communicated to man, the infinite to the finite. God has communicated, in addition, in words that are understandable to us. The One who made man capable of language in the first place has communicated to man in language. Also, God has communicated truth about both spiritual reality and physical reality, about both the nature of God and the nature of man, about both events in past history and events in the future. Where all humanistic systems of thought are unable to give an adequate explanation of things, the Bible as God's statement is adequate.

It is equally important to note that the Bible's answer does not have to be believed blindly. There are good and sufficient reasons for seeing that it is true. It is the key that fits into the lock of what we know best about ourselves and the universe around us.

To change the metaphor: Imagine a book which has been mutilated, leaving just one inch of printed matter on each page. Although it would obviously be impossible to piece together and understand the book's story, few people would imagine that the printing which was left on those one-inch portions had come together by chance. However, if the torn pieces of each page were found in a trunk and were added in the right places, then the story could be read and would make sense.

So it is with Christianity. The ripped pages remaining in the book correspond to the universe and its form and to the mannishness of man. The parts of the pages discovered in the trunk correspond to the Scriptures, which are God's propositional communication to mankind. Neither the universe nor personality can give the answer to the whole meaning of the created order. Yet both are important as a testimony in helping us know that the Scriptures, God's communication to man, are what they claim to be. The question is whether the communication given by God completes and explains the portions we had before and especially whether it explains what was open to observation before (though without an explanation), that is, that the existence of the universe and its form and the mannishness of man are not just chance configurations of the printer's scrambled type.

This illustration is important for several reasons. First, it emphasizes that Christians do not start out from themselves autonomously, as the humanists try to do. God gives the pages, and thus God gives the answers.

Second, it helps us see the proper place of man's reason. Just as a scientist does not create the order in the universe but does recognize it, so reason does not create the answer but simply recognizes it. Of course this does not mean that reason will necessarily *receive* the answer. Each person has to *choose* to receive God's truth. But God's truth is clear. The individual must acknowledge that he (and mankind) is not autonomous, not the center of all things, and he must acknowledge that he has many times done what he knows to be wrong and thus needs the work of Christ for himself. Those who refuse to back down from the position of autonomy make it impossible for themselves to receive the truth, even though there are good and sufficient reasons for knowing that it is the truth.

The Personal Origin of Man

The Scriptures tell us that the universe exists and has form and meaning because it was created purposefully by a personal Creator. This being the case, we see that, as we are personal, we are not something strange and out of line with an otherwise impersonal universe. Since we are made in the image of God, we are in line with God. There is a continuity, in other words, between ourselves, though finite, and the infinite Creator who stands behind the universe as its Creator and its final source of meaning.

Unlike the evolutionary concept of an impersonal beginning plus time plus chance, the Bible gives an account of man's origin as a finite person made in God's image, that is, like God. We see then how man can have personality and dignity and value. Our uniqueness is guaranteed, something which is impossible in the materialistic system. If there is no qualitative distinction between man and other organic life (animals or plants), why should we feel greater concern over the death of a human being than over the death of a laboratory rat? Is man in the end any higher?

Though this is the logical end of the materialistic system, men and women still usually in practice assume that people have some real value. All the way back to the dawn of our investigations in history, we find that man is still man. Wherever we turn, to the caves of the Pyrenees, to the Sumerians in Mesopotamia, and even further back to Neanderthal man's burying his dead in flower petals, it makes no difference: men everywhere show by their art and their accomplishments that they have been and have considered themselves to be unique. They *were* unique, and people today are unique. What is wrong is a world-view which fails to explain that uniqueness. All people are unique because they are made in the image of God.

The Bible tells us also, however, that man is flawed. We see this to be the case both within ourselves and in our societies throughout the world. People are noble and people are cruel; people have heights of moral achievement and depths of moral depravity.

But this is not simply an enigma, nor is it explained in terms of "the animal in man." The Bible explains how man is flawed, without destroying the uniqueness and dignity of man. Man is evil and experiences the results of evil, not because man is non-man but because man is fallen and thus is *abnormal*.

This is the significance of the third chapter of Genesis. Some time after the original Creation (we do not know how long), man rebelled against God. Being made in the image of God as persons, Adam and Eve were able to make real choices. They had true creativity, not just in the area we call "art" but also in the area of choice. And they used this choice to turn from God as their true integration point. Their ability to choose would have been equally validated if they had chosen not to turn away from God, as their true integration point, but instead they used their choice to try to make themselves autonomous. In doing this, they were acting against the moral absolute of the universe, namely, God's character—and thus evil among people was born.

The Fall brought not only moral evil but also the abnormality of (1) each person divided from himself or herself; (2) people divided from other people; (3) mankind divided from nature; and (4) nature divided from nature. This was the consequence of the choice made by Adam and Eve some time after the Creation. It was not any original deformity that made them choose in this way. God had not made them robots, and so they had real choice. It is man, therefore, and not God, who is responsible for evil.

We have to keep pointing out, because the idea is strange to a society by which the Bible has been neglected or distorted, that Christianity does not begin with a statement of Christ as Savior. That comes later in its proper setting. Genesis 1:1 says, "In the beginning God created. . . ." Christianity begins with the personal and infinite God who is the Creator. It goes on to show that man is made in God's image but then tells us that man is now fallen. It is the rebellion of man that has made the world *abnormal*. So there is a broken line as we look back to the creation of man by God. A chasm stands there near the beginning, the chasm which is the Fall, the choice to go against God and His Word.

What follows from this is that not everything that happens in the world is "natural." Unlike modern materialistic thought on both sides of the Iron Curtain, Christianity does not see everything in history as equally "normal." Because of the abnormality brought about by man, not everything which occurs in history should be there. Thus, not all that history brings forth is right just because it happens, and not all personal drives and motives are equally good. Here, then, is a marked difference between Christianity and almost all other philosophies. Most other philosophies do not have the concept of a present abnormality. Therefore, they hold that everything now is normal; things are now as they always have been.

By contrast, Christians do *not* see things as if they always have been this way. This is of immense importance in understanding evil in the world. It is possible for Christians to speak of things as absolutely wrong, for they are not original in human society. They are derived from the Fall; they are in that sense "abnormal." It also means we can stand against what is wrong and cruel without standing against God, for He did not make the world as it now is.

This understanding of the chasm between what mankind and history are now and what they could have been—and should have been, from the way they were made—gives us a real moral framework for life, one which is compatible with our nature and aspirations. So there are "rules for life," like the signs on cliff tops which read: DANGER—KEEP OUT. The signs are there to help, not hinder us. God has put them there because to live in this way, according to His rules, is the way for both safety and fulfillment. The God who made us and knows what is for our best good is the same God who gives us His commands. When we break these, it is not only wrong, it is also not for our best good; it is not for our fulfillment as unique persons made in the image of God.

Freedom Within Form
We should not allow ourselves to hurry past this point, because it is of tremendous importance in relation to the problems we out-

lined in the first three chapters of this book. Knowing what is right and wrong, we have a way to have order and freedom simultaneously. It is relatively easy to attain order in society and not have any freedom. There are plenty of examples of that today. Likewise, it is easy to practice freedom without any order. There are examples of that, too, in the Western societies most of us live in. But how do we get both together? That is the problem.

The Bible gives a world-view that provides order and yet at the same time freedom. God's rules are like a perimeter fence. We must stay within that fence if we are to avoid getting messed up. But inside the fence we have an almost endless *variety of possibilities for freedom*. These touch every area of human life.

A good example is the pursuit of science. The Christian world-view gives us a base for science, yet (since we are made in the image of God) a freedom to pursue science. The birth of modern science is generally conceded to be heavily indebted to the Christian world-view. The Bible tells us that the universe is ordered, because God made it to cohere in all sorts of amazing ways. At the same time it tells us that we are persons. We are able to know what is around us; the subject can know the object.

It may seem rather obvious to say we can know what is around us, for everyone lives like this, day in and day out. We drive the car, use the stove, and so forth. Even though we cannot completely know any single detail of what is around us, we can still have accurate knowledge. This is what makes science possible, too. But, for the materialistic philosophers, this is still a problem.

Why is it that the noises we make from our mouths, for example, "cat," "dog," "glass," "hand," have a correspondence with objects in the outside world? That is the problem with which modern philosophers are still struggling. But within the Christian view the answer is simple and obvious: the world was made that way in the first place. Without the Bible's answer of a personal God who has made the universe—and at the same time persons within it to have a relationship with what has been made—people can still know the objects, *but they do not know why they can know them*.

The Importance of Genesis

So the Bible is the key to understanding the universe and its form and the mannishness of man. Without this key our observations are out of perspective; we do not know what we are looking at.

This being the case, our conclusions about what we are seeing can be massively in error.

Unless we are told about our beginnings, we cannot make sense of our present history. And secular study is incapable of doing that. This is not to say that the study of history and science is irrelevant or useless, but when secular study is finished, the most important questions are left unanswered. It can tell us much of patterns and statistics, but not the reason or meaning or significance of it all. Twentieth-century people know something exists, but have no way of saying what that something amounts to.

This is where the early chapters of Genesis are so important. These chapters give the history that comes before anything that secular historians have been able to ascertain, and *it is this presecular history which gives meaning to mankind's present history*.

Some people mistakenly believe that one can "spiritualize" away the history of the first chapters of Genesis and that this will make no difference. They argue that these chapters are not history but something like parables. This type of thinking depreciates the factual content, which gives information about history and the cosmos. Those who do this sometimes imagine that doing this makes little or no difference. But it changes everything. For these chapters tell us the *why* (the significance and meaning) of all the subsequent history which historians can know through their investigations. These chapters tell us also the *why* of our own personal history.

For this reason we can say that in this sense the early chapters of Genesis are more important than anything else we could have. They are the very foundation on which *all* knowledge rests. So we learn from them that before the creation of the universe, the infinite-personal God existed and that He created the universe (the space-time continuum) by choice, out of nothing. The Creation was not without a cause.

The infinite-personal God was its cause. He chose to create, He willed to create, and "it was"—it came into being.

> You are worthy, our Lord and God,
>   to receive glory and honor and power,
> for you created all things,
>   and by your will they were created
>   and have their being.
>   Revelation 4:11

As we have seen already, we learn also about the fact that man was made "in the image of God," a person, and that then there was a space-time Fall.

All the information given by the Bible flows out of the information given in the early chapters of Genesis. If we are to understand the world as it is and ourselves as we are, we must know the flow of history given in these chapters. Take this away and the flow of history is lost. Take this away and even the death of Christ has no meaning.

So the Bible tells us who we are and who other people are. It tells us how people are differentiated from all other things. We do not need to be confused, as is much of modern mankind, about people's distinction from both animal life and the complicated machines of the second half of the twentieth century. Suddenly people have unique value, and we can understand how it is that each of us is different as a person.

Furthermore, we can see that *all* people are similarly to be distinguished from non-man and that therefore we ourselves must look on others as having great value. Anyone who kills a person is not killing just another member of the same biological species, but one of overwhelming value, one made in the image, the likeness, of God.

Any person, no matter who he or she is—a stranger or a friend, a fellow-believer or someone who is still in rebellion against God, anyone of any age, before or after birth—*any and every person is made after the likeness of God.*

Each man, woman, and child is of great value, not for some ulterior motive such as self-gratification or wealth or power or a sex object or "the good of society" or the maintenance of the gene pool—but simply because of his or her origin.

This flow of history that springs from Genesis has implications for every aspect of our lives. Each of us stands in the flow of history. We know our origin—a lineage more ancient than the Queen of England's or the Pilgrim Fathers'. As we look at ourselves in the flow of space-time reality, we see our origin in Adam and Eve, and we know that God has created every human being in His own image.

CHAPTER FIVE

Truth and History

In the previous chapter we saw that the Bible gives us the explanation for the existence of the universe and its form and for the mannishness of man. Or, to reverse this, we came to see that the universe and its form and the mannishness of man are a testimony to the truth of the Bible. In this chapter we will consider a third testimony: the Bible's openness to verification by historical study.

Christianity involves history. To say only that is already to have said something remarkable, because it separates the Judeo-Christian world-view from almost all other religious thought. It is rooted in history.

The Bible tells us how God communicated with man in history. For example, God revealed Himself to Abraham at a point in time and at a particular geographical place. He did likewise with Moses, David, Isaiah, Daniel and so on. The implications of this are extremely important to us. Because the truth God communicated in the Bible is so tied up with the flow of human events, it is possible by historical study to confirm some of the historical details.

It is remarkable that this possibility exists. Compare the information we have from other continents of that period. We know comparatively little about what happened in Africa or South America or China or Russia or even Europe. We see beautiful remains of temples and burial places, cult figures, utensils, and so forth, but there is not much actual "history" that can be reconstructed, at least not much when compared to that which is possible in the Middle East.

When we look at the material which has been discovered from the Nile to the Euphrates that derives from the 2500-year span before Christ, we are in a completely different situation from that in regard to South America or Asia. The kings of Egypt and Assyria built thousands of monuments commemorating their victories and recounting their different exploits. Whole libraries have been discovered from places like Nuzu and Mari and most recently at Ebla, which give hundreds of thousands of texts relating to the historical details of their time. It is within this geographical area that the Bible is set. So it is possible to find material which bears upon what the Bible tells us.

The Bible purports to give us information on history. Is the history accurate? The more we understand about the Middle East between 2500 B.C. and A.D. 100, the more confident we can be that the information in the Bible is reliable, even when it speaks about the simple things of time and place.[94]

Moses and Joshua
Mount Sinai is one of the most important sites of the entire Bible. It was here that the Hebrew people came shortly after their flight from Egypt. Here God spoke to them through Moses, giving them directions for their life as a newly formed nation and making a covenant with them.[95]

The thing to notice about this epochal moment for Israel is the emphasis on history which the Bible itself makes. Time and time again Moses reminds the people of what has happened on Mount Sinai:

> You came near and stood at the foot of the mountain while it blazed with fire to the very heavens, with black clouds and deep darkness. Then the LORD spoke to you out of the fire. You heard the sound of words but saw no form; there was only a voice.
>
> Deuteronomy 4:11, 12

Moses emphasizes that those alive at the time had actually heard God's direct communication in words. They also were eyewitnesses of what had occurred—they saw the cloud and the mountain burning with fire. They saw and they heard. In the same way they had been eyewitnesses of the remarkable events which had accompanied their escape from Egypt shortly before: "But it was your own eyes that saw all these great things the LORD has done" (Deuteronomy 11:7). Therefore, Moses says, on the basis of what they themselves have seen and heard in their own lifetime, they are not to be afraid of their present or future enemies.

> But do not be afraid of them; remember well what the LORD your God did to Pharaoh and to all Egypt. You saw with your own eyes the great trials, the miraculous signs and wonders, the mighty hand and outstretched arm, with which the LORD your God brought you out. The LORD your God will do the same to all the peoples you now fear.
> Deuteronomy 7:18, 19

On the same basis too, Moses urges them to obey God: "Only be careful, and watch yourselves closely so that you do not forget the things your eyes have seen . . ." (Deuteronomy 4:9).

Thus the people's confidence and trust in God and their obedience to Him are alike rooted in truth that is historical and observable. Therefore, the historical records are subject to factual study; the historical records are not only open to verification but to falsification as well. The relationship between God and His people was not based on an inward experience inside their own heads, but upon a reality which was seen and heard. They were called to obey God not because of a leap of faith, but because of God's real acts in history. For God is the *living* God. The universe within which man lives is not a "closed" system of natural causes. The universe is God's creation and it is "open" to Him. God has acted into history, into a history which is seeable.

"Religious truth" according to the Bible involves the same sort of truth which people operate on in their everyday lives. If something is true, then its opposite cannot also be true. For example, if the Israelites were slaves in Egypt under the Egyptian pharaohs at a particular moment in history, then it cannot also be true that at the same time the Israelites were *not* slaves in Egypt. Likewise, if Jesus was raised from the dead, His body will not be able to be found where He was buried near Jerusalem.

This is the Bible's view of truth: certain things are true whose opposites are not true. It is important to understand that this concept of truth did not begin with the Greeks, as some people suggest. God made the human mind itself so that we all act on this. Even those who deny the concept act on it in practice. If someone says that all truth is relative, he is saying absolutely that this is true. The necessities of everyday life give the lie to relativistic thought.

From the Bible's viewpoint, all truth finally rests upon the fact that the infinite-personal God exists in contrast to His not existing. This means that God exists objectively; He exists whether or not people say He does. The Bible also teaches that God is personal. That means, therefore, that the statements "God does *not* exist" and "God is *im*personal" are false.

Three things should be emphasized about the Hebrew (and biblical) view of truth.

1. In the Hebrew (and biblical) view, truth is grounded ultimately in the existence and character of God and what has been given to us by God in creation and revelation. Because people are finite, reality cannot be exhausted by human reason. Mankind, being limited, can know many things only through revelation. (Biblical truth is bountifully full. Thus, while what the Bible teaches can be put into words and discussed, it so gives things in balance that its teaching as a whole is often richer than any single statement quoted as a proof text.)

2. The biblical view of truth is not a lesser view of truth than the Greek view, but a far higher one. The Judeo-Christian worldview is not merely a philosophic system to be reasoned about abstractly as a nicely balanced system as the Greeks did. It is certainly a world-view, one that makes sense of our experience. But it is more; *it is a world-view related to history* and therefore at crucial points open to confirmation through what can be touched and seen.

3. It is a view of truth that involves the whole person; it is to be enjoyed; it is to be upheld through opposition and denial. It demands choice and commitment. Why? Because it is objectively true. It is truth both to God and to us. Thus, the Hebrew (and biblical) view of truth, rather than being similar to the modern relativistic (or dialetical or existential) concept of truth, is completely contrary to it.

It is within this Judeo-Christian view of truth that, by its own insistence, we must understand the Bible. Moses could appeal to real historical events as the basis for Israel's confidence and obedience into the future. He could even pass down to subsequent generations physical reminders of what God had done, so that the people could see them and remember. So, for example, he gave the Ten Commandments on the two tablets of stone to be kept in the Ark of the Covenant. Likewise he gave them a pot of manna (the food provided by God during the wilderness wanderings), and the rod belonging to Aaron, Moses' brother, which had been used in Egypt and later as a sign of God's power and presence. These were kept as silent witnesses of truth; they were observable in history from generation to generation within the Jewish sanctuary.

At the time of Joshua, who followed Moses in the leadership of the Jews, we find the same emphasis on historic testimony as in the writings of Moses: "Joshua set up the twelve stones that had been in the middle of the Jordan at the spot where the priests who carried the ark of the covenant had stood. And they are there to this day" (Joshua 4:9). God is not an abstract force or idea. Man's experience of God is not just within his head. God is active in history. And just as in the time of Moses God commanded various items to be kept as physical reminders of what He had done, so God did the same thing in the time of Joshua.

God temporarily dried up the Jordan River so that the Jews could pass. As a memorial of that fact—so that it could be observed through subsequent generations—two piles of twelve stones each were made. The first pile was made in the riverbed of the Jordan itself while the people were actually crossing. There they could be seen for centuries when the water in the Jordan was low. The second pile was made out of rocks which the Jews lifted from the river as they passed by and then piled on the dry land at their camp in Gilgal: "And Joshua set up at Gilgal the twelve stones they had taken out of Jordan" (Joshua 4:20).[96]

Abraham and Isaac

The Bible's account of Abraham's life also emphasizes historic events as real events. This becomes especially obvious—and important—in the account of Abraham's "sacrifice" of his son, Isaac.

The Bible sets this event in a definite framework. We are told, for example, that Abraham was directed by God to take Isaac to a particular mountain, Mount Moriah—a long three-day journey from where Abraham and Isaac were. This is important, not just an incidental detail. This was the site on which Solomon many years later built the temple. And the New Testament tells us that Jesus died not far from this same spot.

None of this is by chance. Jesus died as the promised Lamb of

God, as John the Baptist calls Him. He died to take away the sin of the world. As such He is the fulfillment of what was prefigured in the "almost sacrifice" of Isaac a bit less than 2,000 years earlier. And as such, too, Jesus is the fulfillment of all the sacrifices associated with the tabernacle and temple. God was indicating in "the sacrifice of Isaac" that it is not an animal which delivers people from their sins, but a Person.

This also helps us to understand why something which the rest of the Bible tells us is abhorrent to God, human sacrifice, could have been used as the supreme test of Abraham's trust in God's promises to him. It was not because God wished Isaac to die (and, of course, Isaac did not die), but because God wished to make clear that He Himself would provide the sacrifice and that that sacrifice would not be an animal but a very special *Person*.

Let us notice in particular that God did not ask Abraham for a "leap of faith," any more than He asked the people of Israel for a leap of faith at the time of Moses. Abraham had already been given many evidences of God's reality and of His reliability. God had spoken to him over and over again before this time:

The Lord had said to Abram, "Leave your country, your people and your father's household and go to the land I will show you.

"I will make you into a great nation
    and I will bless you;
I will make your name great,
    and you will be a blessing.
I will bless those who bless you,
    and whoever curses you I will curse;
and all peoples on earth
    will be blessed through you."
                                  Genesis 12:1-3

Then again, when Abraham came into Canaan: "The LORD said to Abram after Lot had parted from him, 'Lift up your eyes from where you are and look north and south, east and west. All the land that you see I will give to you and your offspring forever . . .'" (Genesis 13:14, 15).

God promised to give Abraham a new country and descendants. However, where was the son and heir? Abraham was old, and in his concern to provide an heir he had first chosen a servant called Eliezer who came from Damascus. Here are the key passages from Genesis which record Abraham's experience in getting a proper heir:

Then the word of the LORD came to him: "This man will not be your heir, but a son coming from your own body will be your heir." He took him outside and said, "Look at the heavens and count the stars—if indeed you can count them." Then he said to him, "So shall your offspring be."

Abram believed the LORD, and he credited it to him as righteousness.

Genesis 15:4-6

When Abram was ninety-nine years old, the LORD appeared to him and said, "I am God Almighty; walk before me and be blameless. I will confirm my covenant between me and you and will greatly increase your numbers."

Abram fell facedown, and God said to him, "As for me, this is my covenant with you: You will be the father of many nations. No longer will you be called Abram; your name will be Abraham, for I have made you a father of many nations."

Genesis 17:1-5

The LORD appeared to Abraham near the great trees of Mamre while he was sitting at the entrance to his tent in the heat of the day. Abraham looked up and saw three men standing nearby. When he saw them, he hurried from the entrance of his tent to meet them and bowed low to the ground.

He said, "If I have found favor in your eyes, my lord, do not pass your servant by. . . ."

"Where is your wife Sarah?" they asked him.

"There, in the tent," he said.

Then the LORD said, "I will surely return to you about this time next year, and Sarah your wife will have a son."

Now Sarah was listening at the entrance to the tent, which was behind him. Abraham and Sarah were already old and well advanced in years, and Sarah was past the age of childbearing. So Sarah laughed to herself as she thought, "After I am worn out and my master is old, will I now have this pleasure?"

Then the LORD said to Abraham, "Why did Sarah laugh and say, 'Will I really have a child, now that I am old?' Is anything too hard for the LORD? I will return to you at the appointed time next year and Sarah will have a son."

Genesis 18:1-3, 9-14

Thus, in this remarkable way Abraham came to have an heir, just as God had said. Abraham also saw God's remarkable deliverance of his nephew Lot from Sodom and Gomorroh.

Therefore, the certainty that God was both real and trustworthy had been established to Abraham through a number of revelations and events. He had heard God, he had talked with Him, he had received propositional revelation from God. He had seen God keep His promises, both in regard to a son (even though he and Sarah were old) and in regard to Lot's rescue. When we read the following account of the "sacrifice" of Isaac, we must keep these facts in mind. Abraham knew God was both real and trustworthy.

> Some time later God tested Abraham. He said to him, "Abraham!"
> "Here I am," he replied.
> Then God said, "Take your son, your only son Isaac, whom you love, and go to the region of Moriah. Sacrifice him there as a burnt offering on one of the mountains I will tell you about."
> Early the next morning Abraham got up and saddled his donkey. He took with him two of his servants and his son Isaac. When he had cut enough wood for the burnt offering, he set out for the place God had told him about. On the third day Abraham looked up and saw the place in the distance. He said to his servants, "Stay here with the donkey while I and the boy go over there. We will worship and then we will come back to you."
> Abraham took the wood for the burnt offering and placed it on his son Isaac, and he himself carried the fire and the knife. As the two of them went on together, Isaac spoke up and said to his father Abraham, "Father?"
> "Yes, my son?" Abraham replied.
> "The fire and wood are here," Isaac said, "but where is the lamb for the burnt offering?"
> Abraham answered, "God himself will provide the lamb for the burnt offering, my son." And the two of them went on together.
> When they reached the place God had told him about, Abraham built an altar there and arranged the wood on it. He bound his son Isaac and laid him on the altar, on top of the wood. Then he reached out his hand and took the knife to slay his son. But the angel of the LORD called out to him from heaven, "Abraham! Abraham!"
> "Here I am," he replied.
> "Do not lay a hand on the boy," he said. "Do not do anything to him. Now I know that you fear God, because you have not withheld from me your son, your only son."
> Abraham looked up and there in a thicket he saw a ram caught by its horns. He went over and took the ram and sacrificed it as a burnt offering instead of his son. So Abraham called that place "The LORD will provide." And to this day it is said, "On the mountain of the LORD it will be provided."
>
> Genesis 22:1-14

Far from Abraham being asked to make a blind leap of faith, the

Bible indicates that it would have been unreasonable and disobedient on Abraham's part for him not to obey God. He had previously had ample evidence of God's reliability. Therefore he had said to the servants, with real assurance, ". . . we will come back to you" (Genesis 22:5).

This is not to minimize his difficulty as a human father, as he stood there with his much loved son at his side. Nor is it to minimize the profound obedience he showed toward God as he followed along toward the sacrifice of that son until God stopped him. But any idea that Abraham's faith was contrary to reason overlooks all that had gone before.

Paul in Corinth

This emphasis—that faith is not contrary to reason—is presented in both the Old and the New Testaments. The entire Bible makes plain that the history it records is to be seen as real history. Consider the Apostle Paul in Greece. Paul visited Corinth and stayed there for a year and a half.

> There he met a Jew named Aquila, a native of Pontus, who had recently come from Italy with his wife Priscilla, because Claudius had ordered all the Jews to leave Rome. Paul went to see them, and because he was a tentmaker as they were, he stayed and worked with them. Every Sabbath he reasoned in the synagogue, trying to persuade Jews and Greeks. . . . So Paul stayed for a year and a half, teaching them the word of God.
>
> Acts 18:2-4, 11

We have now left far behind the great powers of Assyria and Babylon and Egypt. Alexander the Great has also come and gone. Though the Greek language is still used through the Mediterranean world, it is now Rome who rules and Claudius who is emperor. This is our setting; we are in a real moment of history and the people we read about in the Bible are as real as ourselves.[97]

There are a number of interesting things about Corinth. We learn from Acts 18:2 that while Paul was here he met a Jewish couple, Priscilla and Aquila, who had recently come from Italy, and he stayed with them and, in fact, supported himself financially by helping them in their craft of tentmaking. Priscilla and Aquila had had to leave Italy, Acts tells us, because Claudius had commanded all Jews to depart from Rome.

What we should notice is that the Book of Acts gives us here, in the midst of an account of Paul's preaching in Corinth and his trials and deliverances, a statement about the Roman Emperor Claudius and a decree of his against the Jews. We are immediately conscious that this is the same type of world-view we have become accustomed to throughout the Old Testament. This is real history again.

The Roman biographer Suetonius tells us more about that expulsion of the Jews, and the occasion can be dated from another source to the year A.D. 49. Acts tells us that the governor in Corinth while Paul was there was a man named Gallio. Now Gallio was a famous man, the brother of Seneca, who was a prominent Roman philosopher and writer and who later became tutor to the future emperor Nero. Seneca wrote about his brother Gallio, and some of his letters have been preserved down to the present. He mentioned, for example, Gallio's year of office in Corinth. This has also been attested by several fragments of an inscribed stone from Delphi (which is across the isthmus from Corinth). This gives the dates when Gallio held his governorship: the summer of A.D. 51 to the summer of A.D. 52. It also gives his title as "Proconsul of Achaia" (that is, southern Greece), which is exactly the title used of him in Acts 18:12.

Here, then, are a number of historical strands inside and outside the Bible which run together naturally and easily. Archaeology has even identified the governor's palace at Corinth, and we can see the very place where Paul is likely to have appeared before Gallio. [98]

Resurrection and History

Later we find Paul writing a letter to the church at Corinth. In it he presents what he preached and taught throughout the Roman Empire:

> Now, brothers, I want to remind you of the gospel I preached to you, which you received and on which you have taken your stand. By this gospel you are saved, if you hold firmly to the word I preached to you. Otherwise, you have believed in vain.
>
> For what I received I passed on to you as of first importance: that Christ died for our sins according to the Scriptures, that he was buried, that he was raised on the third day according to the Scriptures, and that he appeared to Peter, and then to the Twelve. After that, he appeared to more than five hundred of the brothers at the same time, most of whom are still living, though some have fallen asleep. Then

he appeared to James, then to all the apostles, and last of all he appeared to me also, as to one abnormally born.

For I am the least of the apostles and do not even deserve to be called an apostle, because I persecuted the church of God. But by the grace of God I am what I am, and his grace to me was not without effect. No, I worked harder than all of them—yet not I, but the grace of God that was with me. Whether, then, it was I or they, this is what we preach, and this is what you believed.

But if it is preached that Christ has been raised from the dead, how can some of you say that there is no resurrection of the dead? If there is no resurrection of the dead, then not even Christ has been raised. And if Christ has not been raised, our preaching is useless and so is your faith. More than that, we are then found to be false witnesses about God, for we have testified about God that he raised Christ from the dead. But he did not raise him if in fact the dead are not raised. For if the dead are not raised, then Christ has not been raised either. And if Christ has not been raised, your faith is futile; you are still in your sins. Then those who have fallen asleep in Christ are lost. If only for this life we have hope in Christ, we are to be pitied more than all men.

But Christ has indeed been raised from the dead, the firstfruits of those who have fallen asleep. For since death came through a man, the resurrection of the dead comes also through a man. For as in Adam all die, so in Christ all will be made alive. But each in his own turn: Christ, the firstfruits; then, when he comes, those who belong to him. Then the end will come, when he hands over the kingdom to God the Father after he has destroyed all dominion, authority and power.

1 Corinthians 15:1-24

In this section of his First Letter to the Corinthians, Paul asserts unequivocally that Jesus has been raised from the tomb and that we shall ourselves be raised like Him in the future. Jesus' body was placed in the tomb, but it did not remain there. Jesus rose from the dead. It was not simply a subjective experience by which the disciples were deceived. Jesus rose from the dead as a space-time fact and then He appeared to the disciples.

But we should notice particularly the other side of Paul's argument. He says, "Suppose that Jesus did *not* rise from the dead." That is not what he believes, of course, for he knows on objective grounds that Jesus has been raised; he himself had met Jesus and heard Him speak to him in the Hebrew language. And there were many other eyewitnesses to the resurrected Christ. Paul is saying, "Let us just suppose for the sake of seeing what follows that Jesus was not resurrected. What would happen then?" Paul is quick to reply: "If this did not happen, everything is finished from Christianity's point of view. We may as well 'eat and drink, for tomorrow we die.' If Christ did not rise from the dead as a historical fact, we have no Savior. Therefore we are 'still in our sins'; we shall have to face God's judgment and bear the penalty for our sin alone."

What he does *not* say is the sort of thing one hears all over the world today from churchmen who have been influenced by existential thought. They say, "Even if Jesus did *not* rise from the dead, Christianity is untouched." One such theologian said that the Resurrection took place—but if a television crew had visited the tomb that morning, it could not have recorded the event. In other words, the body of Christ was still there! But this is unthinkable to Paul. Either Christ rose from the dead as an objective fact of history, or He did not. If He did not, Christianity is finished.

When we examine the actual account of the Resurrection of Jesus in the Gospels, we find the same emphasis. The Garden Tomb in Jerusalem may not be the precise place where Jesus was buried, but certainly it must have been a tomb very like it and somewhere near that site. On the third day after the burial, Jesus rose from the dead. Here is how the Gospel of John records the events:

> Early on the first day of the week, while it was still dark, Mary of Magdala went to the tomb and saw that the stone had been removed from the entrance. . . . Then Simon Peter, who was behind him [the other disciple, John] arrived and went into the tomb. He saw the strips of linen lying there, as well as the burial cloth that had been around Jesus' head. The cloth was folded up by itself, separate from the linen.
>
> John 20:1, 6, 7

Notice that Mary Magdalene and Peter and John observed something *with normal observation*—the stone was rolled away; the linen cloth and the headcloth in which Jesus had been wrapped at His burial were still lying in the empty tomb. We read in Luke 24 that Jesus later appeared to all the disciples as they were gathered together. Evidently they were in some agitation, both from what they had witnessed at Christ's death and by the reports that Jesus had risen from the dead:

> While they were still talking about this, Jesus himself stood among them and said to them, "Peace be with you."

They were startled and frightened, thinking they saw a ghost. He said to them, "Why are you troubled, and why do doubts rise in your minds? Look at my hands and my feet. It is I myself! Touch me and see; a ghost does not have flesh and bones, as you see I have."

When he had said this, he showed them his hands and feet. And while they still did not believe it because of joy and amazement, he asked them, "Do you have anything here to eat?" They gave him a piece of broiled fish, and He took it and ate it in their presence.

Luke 24:36-43

The Resurrection of Christ is presented in the Gospels as verifiable history. It is given in the same frame of reference as applies in science—when Christ arose, He did not leave His body in the grave. The Resurrection was open to normal observation. There were the graveclothes. Jesus spoke to the disciples. He could be touched. He ate before them.

Thomas and the Resurrected Christ

Perhaps the most striking incident recorded involves Thomas:

Now Thomas (called Didymus), one of the Twelve, was not with the disciples when Jesus came. When the other disciples told him that they had seen the Lord, he declared, "Unless I see the nail marks in his hands and put my finger where the nails were, and put my hand into his side, I will not believe it."

A week later his disciples were in the house again, and Thomas was with them. Though the doors were locked, Jesus came and stood among them and said, "Peace be with you!" Then he said to Thomas, "Put your finger here; see my hands. Reach out your hand and put it into my side. Stop doubting and believe."

Thomas said to him, "My Lord and my God!"

Then Jesus told him, "Because you have seen me, you have believed; blessed are those who have not seen and yet have believed."

John 20:24-29

Just as Moses said, well over a thousand years before, "You saw, you heard," so the Gospels say, "You saw, you heard!" God acted in history, and this was observed and was able to be described in ordinary language.

If Jesus did not live, or if He did not rise from the dead, Christianity cannot continue. It cannot live on as a mere *idea,* because Christianity is about objective truth and not merely religious experiences. Both the Old Testament and the New Testament claim to be truth, in contrast to that which is not true, and this truth is rooted in history. We have only one hope, and it rests on a serious commitment to the existence of God and the reliability of His Word, the Bible, in all the areas in which it speaks.

There is truth that can be known and before which we can bow with joy—truth that in a very real way is climaxed in the physical Resurrection of Christ. If the tomb was not empty—so that a camera crew could have recorded the absence of Jesus' body at the same time that they could have filmed the linen strips and head-cloth in which His body had been wrapped—we have no hope.

Thomas should have believed on the basis of the evidence that he had from the other disciples and that was quite sufficient. Jesus rebuked him when He appeared to him and said, "Put your finger here; see my hands. Reach out your hand and put it into my side. Stop doubting and believe." After Thomas had said, "My Lord and my God!" Jesus said, "Because you have seen me, you have believed; blessed are those who have not seen and yet have believed."

Is Jesus saying by this that believing is a blind leap of un-grounded faith? Quite the opposite! Because Thomas insisted on seeing and touching Jesus in His resurrected body, we have been given in the Gospels an even clearer evidence of the Resurrection than we would otherwise have had. But Jesus is saying that Thomas should have believed without this additional evidence, be-cause the evidence available to Thomas before was in itself suffi-cient. In other words, before Thomas saw and heard Jesus in this way, he was in the same position as we are today. Both he at that time and we today have the same sufficient witness of those who have seen and heard and who have had the opportunity to touch the resurrected Christ. In fact, in the light of this sufficient and sure witness we, like Thomas, are disobedient if we do not bow. We are without excuse.

After telling about Thomas, the Gospel of John then turns to another appearance of Jesus:

> Afterward Jesus appeared again to his disciples by the Sea of Tiber-ias. It happened this way: Simon Peter, Thomas (called Didymus), Nathanael from Cana in Galilee, the sons of Zebedee, and two other disciples were together. "I'm going out to fish," Simon Peter told them, and they said, "We'll go with you." So they went out and got into the boat, but that night they caught nothing.
>
> Early in the morning, Jesus stood on the shore, but the disciples did not realize that it was Jesus.

He called out to them, "Friends, haven't you [caught] any fish?"
"No," they answered.

He said, "Throw your net on the right side of the boat and you will find some." When they did, they were unable to haul the net in because of the large number of fish.

Then the disciple whom Jesus loved said to Peter, "It is the Lord!" As soon as Simon Peter heard him say, "It is the Lord," he wrapped his outer garment around him (for he had taken it off) and jumped into the water. The other disciples followed in the boat, towing the net full of fish, for they were not far from the shore, about a hundred yards. When they landed, they saw a fire of burning coals there with fish on it, and some bread.

Jesus said to them, "Bring some of the fish you have just caught."

Simon Peter climbed aboard and dragged the net ashore. It was full of large fish, 153, but even with so many the net was not torn. Jesus said to them, "Come and have breakfast." None of the disciples dared ask him, "Who are you?" They knew it was the Lord. Jesus came, took the bread and gave it to them, and did the same with the fish. This was now the third time Jesus appeared to his disciples after he was raised from the dead.

John 21:1-14

The resurrected Jesus stood there on the beach of the Sea of Galilee. Before the disciples reached the store, He had already prepared a fire with fish cooking on it for them to eat. It was a fire that could be seen and felt; it cooked the fish, and the fish and bread could be eaten for breakfast.

When the fire died down, it left ashes on the beach; the disciples were well fed with bread and fish. There is no reason to suppose that Christ's footprints were not visible on the beach.

We must respond with Thomas: "My Lord and my God!"

CHAPTER SIX

Our Personal Response and Social Action

The relationship of Chapters 4, 5, and 6 to Chapters 1, 2, and 3 is direct and far-reaching. In the flood of the loss of humanness in our age—including the flow from abortion-on-demand to infanticide and on to euthanasia—the only thing that can stem this tide is the certainty of the absolute uniqueness and value of people. And the only thing which gives us this is the knowledge that people are made in the image of God. We have no other final protection. And the only way we know that people are made in the image of God is through the Bible and the Incarnation of Christ, which we know from the Bible.

If people are not made in the image of God, the pessimistic, realistic humanist is right: the human race is indeed an abnormal wart on the smooth face of a silent and meaningless universe. In this setting, abortion, infanticide, and euthanasia (including the killing of mentally deranged criminals, the severely handicapped, or the elderly who are an economic burden) are completely logical. Any person can be obliterated for what society at one moment thinks of as its own social or economic good. Without the Bible and without the revelation in Christ (which is only told to us in the Bible) there is nothing to stand between us and our children and the eventual acceptance of the monstrous inhumanities of the age.

In Chapters 4 and 5 we saw reasons why we can know that the Bible is truth. The existence of the universe and its form and the uniqueness of man testify to the truth of Scripture, and historical study likewise testifies to the truth of Scripture. The Bible gives us a solid and certain basis on which we can begin to act toward stemming the side of inhumanity. The solution to the inhuman drift begins, however, with each of us as individuals. It begins with you, with me—with each of us.

First Steps Toward Solving the Problem

First, Christianity must be acknowledged to be the truth. Christianity and Christ must not be accepted merely to change society and stop the drift of our culture toward the loss of humanness.

Unhappily, it is possible for people to reject the truth of Christianity and the claims of Christ and yet to hope that others will accept Christianity so that the drift of society will be halted. They think that some kind of Christian revival would be useful in order to affect human behavior and thus protect their own political and economic comfort, allowing them to keep their personal peace and affluence. Biblical Christianity and Christ will indeed stop the drift, but not if Christianity is only used for manipulation by those who think it is not true—but only useful.

In contrast to this attempted utilitarian use of Christianity, what must we do? First, we should see that, for what are good and sufficient reasons, Christianity is true. Then we should personally bow as finite creatures before our infinite-personal Creator. And then we should accept Christ as Savior to remove our personal moral guilt before God. We need that true moral guilt removed because there is the absolute of the Creator's character, and over and over again we have deliberately done what we know to be wrong.

God's promise of a solution to mankind's revolt against Him was first given in the third chapter of Genesis. This promise was expanded with increasing clarity right through the Old Testament. A Messiah, a Savior, was coming. He would take upon Himself the punishment of our sins. As Isaiah said, some 700 years before Christ came:

> We all, like sheep, have gone astray,
> each of us has turned to his own way;

and the Lord has laid on him
the iniquity of us all.

Isaiah 53:6

And we are told that the work of Christ as the dying and resurrected Lamb of God was sufficient to reconcile us to God, that we do not have to add any "works" of our own, that we are saved by the infinite value of what Christ has done—plus *nothing*. Salvation is a gift that we receive with empty hands. This is what it means to have faith in Christ, or to accept Christ as Savior.

The Lordship of Christ

But when we accept Christ as Savior, we must also acknowledge and then act upon the fact that if He is our Savior, He is also our Lord in *all* of life. He is Lord not just in religious things and not just in cultural things such as art and music, but in our intellectual lives and in business and our attitude toward the devaluation of people's humanness in our culture. Acknowledging Christ's Lordship and placing ourselves under what is taught in the whole Bible includes thinking and acting as citizens in relation to our government and its laws. We must know what those laws are and act responsibly to help to change them if they do not square with the Bible's concepts of justice and humanness. The biblical answers have to be lived and not just thought.

We must live under the Lordship of Christ in all the areas of life—at great cost, if need be. It is moving to think of the Christians in China, paying a great price for their loyalty to Christ, but that does not relieve each of us from being under the Lordship of Christ in regard to our own country.

Who is on the cutting edge here? The doctor who pays the price of having certain hospitals closed to him because he will not perform abortions. The businessman who knows he is forfeiting advancement in his company because he will not go along with some inhuman practice of his company. The professor of sociology who is willing to lose his post because he will not teach sociology on the basis of determinism. The pastor who loses his church rather than follow the dictates of a liberal theology or a "trashy Christianity." Or the pastor who preaches the Bible, stressing that today's people are called to sacrificial action, rather than keeping his congregation comfortable while death, spiritual and physical, is built up year after year for their children and grandchildren. Examples could be endlessly multiplied.

Faithfulness to the Lordship of Christ means using the constitutional processes while we still have them. We live in a shrinking island of free constitutional practice. Only a small percentage of countries in the world still possess this. The Lordship of Christ means using these processes to speak and to act on the basis of the principles set forth in the Bible.

With Christ as Savior and Lord, we must do all we can to lead others to Christ. And simultaneously we must use every constitutional practice to offset the rise of authoritarian governments and the loss of humanness in our society. But there is no use in talking of offsetting the loss of humanness in society if we do not act humanly to all people about us in the contacts of our individual lives. We must practice the human alternatives set forth at the end of Chapter 3. We ourselves must act humanly, even when it is costly.

We implore those of you who are Christians to exert all your influence to fight against the increasing loss of humanness— through legislation, social action, and other means at your disposal, both privately and publicly, individually and collectively, in all areas of your lives.

Without the uniqueness and inherent dignity of each human being, no matter how old or young, sick or well, resting on the fact that each person is made in the image of God, there is no sufficient foundation to build on as we resist the loss of humanness in our generation. So we would say again to those of you who are Christians, do not allow your only base, your only hope to be able to stand—namely, the Bible—to be weakened by however subtle means. The Bible is truth in all its parts, and provides, if taken as a whole, the truth of salvation and also a base to work from in our daily lives, a base to stand on morally.

So we who are Christians must, on the one hand, fight with determination and sacrifice for the individual in society, and on the other, provide the loving care of people as individuals. Thus the world will truly feel our presence in its midst as the true salt of the earth. That salt will be a true preservative, both showing forth the beauty of care in the midst of utilitarian ugliness and also helping to remove the festering malignancy of evil that surrounds us.

The Challenge Before Us

As a result of being made in the image of God, each man and woman has a conscience. That built-in monitor, coupled with the advantages of being raised in a society that has had until recently a Judeo-Christian tradition, permits the understanding of the worth of human life to surface periodically, even subconsciously—as, for example, in the recent preoccupation with the special needs of the handicapped adult. But that memory will not last forever without the Judeo-Christian base. Recent history shows us that the conscience can be so corrupted and manipulated that today's unthinkable becomes tomorrow's thinkable with remarkable speed.

People are special and human life is sacred, whether or not we admit it. Every life is precious and worthwhile in itself—not only to us human beings but also to God. Every person is worth fighting for, regardless of whether he is young or old, sick or well, child or adult, born or unborn, or brown, red, yellow, black, or white.

If, in this last part of the twentieth century, the Christian community does not take a prolonged and vocal stand for the dignity of the individual and each person's right to life—for the right of each individual to be treated as created in the image of God, rather than as a collection of molecules with no unique value—we feel that as Christians we have failed the greatest moral test to be put before us in this century.

Future generations will look back, and many will either scoff or believe in Christ on the basis of whether we Christians of today took a sacrificial stand in our various walks of life on these overwhelmingly important issues. If we do not take a stand here and now, we certainly cannot lay any claim to being the salt of the earth in our generation. We are neither preserving moral values and the dignity of the individual nor showing compassion for our fellow human beings.

Will future generations look back and remember that—even if the twentieth century *did* end with a great surge of inhumanity—at least there was one group who stood consistently, whatever the price, for the value of the individual, thus passing on some hope to future generations? Or are we Christians going to be merely swept along with the trends—our own moral values becoming increasingly befuddled, our own apathy reflecting the apathy of the world around us, our own inactivity sharing the inertia of the masses around us, our own leadership becoming soft?

What can we do concerning these issues that we are not doing now?

On the basis of an unweakened Bible, we must teach and act, in our individual lives and as citizens, on the fact that every individual has unique value as made in the image of God. This is so from a child just conceived in the womb to the old with their last gasping breath and beyond; for death does not bring the cessation of life, but all people will spend eternity somewhere . . . with God or not, depending on their relationship to Christ as Savior.

If we ache and have compassion for humanity today in our own country and across the world, we must do all that we can to help people see the truth of Christianity and accept Christ as Savior. And we must stand against the loss of humanness in all its forms. It is God's life-changing power that is able to touch every individual, who then has a responsibility to touch the world around him with the absolutes found in the Bible. In the end we must realize that the tide of humanism, with its loss of humanness, is not merely a cultural ill, but a spiritual ill that the truth given us in the Bible and Christ alone can cure.

CHAPTER SEVEN

How Can We Help?

We Can Make a Difference

The first thing we must realize is that we *can* make a difference in our society. We can change our values and our laws to reflect the sanctity of every human life. Often we look at the money and resources of the proabortion movement (e.g., Planned Parenthood receives over 70 million in tax dollars annually) and are convinced that nothing could stop them. Indeed, in 1973 when the Supreme Court ruled on *Roe vs. Wade,* and brought legalized abortion to America, they were convinced nothing could stop them. Abortion was legal and the issue was put to rest. Yet today abortion remains the hottest moral issue of our time. It receives national media coverage and has elected or defeated several members of Congress. This happened only because a concerned group of citizens took the time and energy to band together to oppose the Supreme Court's decision. They began educating their friends and family. They took the time to picket abortion mills, write letters to the editors of their local papers and speak out about the atrocity of abortion. They voted and worked hard to elect prolife candidates to state and federal legislatures. It was individuals that made the difference and forced the abortion issue out into the open. Today we do have legalized abortion. But we have come a long way toward our goal of changing the laws—and all because a small group decided they would devote themselves to human life. Individuals *do* make a difference.

That is where we begin today: with you as an individual. Educate yourself, your family, and your neighbors about abortion, infanticide, and euthanasia. Tell them the facts about the developing unborn child. Explain to them the medical and legal case for the unborn child. You will be surprised at how little people really know about these issues. Opinions are often formed on the basis of emotion, or with only a minimum of information. Seek to educate yourself and others with the complete facts about these life issues. They speak for themselves.

Secondly, work within your neighborhood and community to stop abortion and promote programs that affirm the sanctity of life. Read your newspapers and begin a "letters to the editor" campaign with your local paper. Perhaps your newspaper has a proabortion bias. Take the time to meet your editor and talk with him about your concerns. Provide him with some of the excellent prolife material that is available. Let him know that you expect to see "the other side" presented in his paper.

Work within your schools to educate young people—particularly teenagers—with the facts about abortion, infanticide, and euthanasia. Planned Parenthood has been tremendously effective at presenting their proabortion propaganda in thousands of schools across the nation. One group of citizens in the state of Washington has put together an alternative package of material to be presented in high schools in their area. Psychologists, social workers, teachers, and parents have developed a curriculum that stresses chastity instead of guilt-free sex and easy access to abortion. This is one way of working to educate young people about these issues and insuring that we do not lose a generation to the anti-life attitudes of our society.

Churches present another opportunity for education about the life issues. Arrange for an adult Sunday school class to discuss these issues. Provide speakers for special seminars and Sunday evening services. The Christian Action Council has developed a special worship service centered around the sanctity of life to be used by churches during a special "Respect Life" Sunday.

Become aware of special events, seminars, and forums in your community where a prolife voice might be needed. Recently in

Chicago a television talk show centering on the life issues was aired. Many prolife people took the time to be in the audience for the television taping. Their questions during the discussion on the show provided viewers with a life-affirming perspective on the issues that was desperately needed. Without their input, thousands of viewers would have been left with only one side of the issues—the anti-life side. Little things make a difference. If you take the time, you will make a difference in your local community. We will stop the destruction of human lives when individuals take the extra time and energy to educate others, and seek to provide life-giving solutions to the problems we face.

In the political arena there is much work that can be done. State right to life organizations have been very effective in organizing voters to work for the election of prolife candidates. The National Right to Life Committee has developed a comprehensive voter identification program to help identify and organize prolife voters in various communities. You can be involved in helping mobilize the prolife voters in your own community. Citizens in many states have learned to draft prolife legislation at the state level. Working with lawyers and legislators, they have learned the law-making process and are able to effectively plan and promote pieces of legislation that will protect lives in their state.

At the national level much the same work is being done. The prolife lobby in Congress has grown and developed over the past decade, thanks to the work of concerned individuals. Local prolife people have worked as precinct captains and campaign workers to help get the voters to put their candidate in Congress. The 1980 elections were only one example of what concerned citizens can do when they effectively mobilize and work in the political arena.

But as one friend has said, being prolife means more than being anti-abortion! We cannot neglect the thousands of pregnant women who need our help to have their babies. In our society, the unwed mother or the teenage girl who elects to have her baby is an example of courage and strength to us all. Many times these girls are forced out of their homes by parents who tell them, "Abortion or else." They need our love, care, and practical help. Organizations like Birthright and Aid for Women provide a home, baby clothes, and a friend to talk things over with. Many more people are needed to volunteer their time and love for these women. The Christian Action Council has developed Crisis Pregnancy Centers in cooperation with local churches. These centers provide women with the shelter and guidance they need during their pregnancy and afterwards. In a society where abortion is the easy answer, these women need our extra support and reassurance that they are loved and that their baby is special.

Parents with special children need our extra help also. Perhaps you have a special child in your own church family. One project could be to arrange a schedule of several times during the week when church members could work with the child and give parents a much-needed break for a few hours. It's a wonderful way to become involved in the child's life, and the rewards will be infinitely greater for you than any possible sacrifice.

These are only a few of the ways that we can make a difference for life in our society. The important thing to remember is that the resources are available for us today. Organizations and individuals have been working for years to protect human lives. Many of them have written about their ideas, and that information is available to you. Educational pamphlets for every level of interest, legal advice from attorneys working full-time on these issues, and information on beginning a Crisis Pregnancy Center are all available for the asking. There is nothing to stop all of us from becoming aware and educated on all the life issues.

Oftentimes people ask how they can help. There is no one way to help bring back the sanctity of life in our society. There are many ways to be involved, depending on your time, circumstances, and resources. Picketing abortion clinics and abortion hospitals is a good way of making it hard for society to ignore the killing. Providing positive alternatives for women and parents involved is important. But above all, *we must never be silent.* The point is that everyone *can* be involved and it will take all our help to stop this destruction of human lives. When a person becomes interested and takes the time to obtain the information, they will find ways to put that information to work in their own sphere of influence. There is no end to the ways in which we all can work to protect the dignity of every human life.

Organizations and Information

Listed below are some of the prolife organizations across the nation. Many of them are general organizations, and many others specialize in a particular part of the battle for human life. Also listed are several books, articles, and journals worth reading and digesting.

Ad Hoc Committee in Defense of Life
8810 National Press Building
Washington, D.C. 20045

American Citizens Concerned for Life
6127 Excelsior Blvd.
Minneapolis, MN 55416

The Pro-life Action League
6369 N. Le Mai Ave.
Chicago, IL 60676

O.M.E.G.A.
P.O. Box 11796
Ft. Lauderdale, FL 33306

The Action League and O.M.E.G.A. specialize in picketing clinics and caring for pregnant women. They will help organize new groups.

The Christian Action Council
422 C Street NE
Washington, D.C. 20002

The CAC is the largest national evangelical prolife organization in the nation. In addition to a very effective lobbying program on Capitol Hill, they have opened over twenty-five Crisis Pregnancy Centers across the nation to help women carry their babies until birth and care for them afterwards. They also publish an excellent newsletter, *Action Line*. All inquiries and requests for information can be directed to Rev. Curtis Young, Executive Director.

The National Right to Life Committee
419 Seventh St., NW, Suite 402
Washington, D.C. 20004

The NRLC has become the premier grassroots organization. They have worked hard to develop chapters in every state. Their Voter Identification Survey is used in every state to help identify and mobilize prolife voters. In addition they publish an excellent prolife paper, *The National Right to Life News.* It is packed with information and helpful articles. The *NRLC News* is a great way to keep current on all the human life issues.

National Youth Prolife Coalition
235 Massachusetts Ave. NE
Washington, D.C. 20002

National Committee for a Human Life Amendment
1707 L Street NW
Suite 400
Washington, D.C. 20036

The group is affiliated with the United States Catholic Conference and is devoted to working in the political arena for passage of a human life amendment.

Life Amendment Political Action Committee
P.O. Box 14263
Ben Franklin Station
Washington, D.C. 20044

This organization has become very influential in working for passage of a variety of prolife legislation in Congress.

American Association of Prolife Obstetricians and Gynecologists
266 Pine Ave.
Lauderdale-by-the-Sea, FL 33303

Baptists for Life
P.O. Box 394
Hallettsville, TX 77964

Lutherans for Life
275 N. Syndicate
Box 988
St. Paul, MN 55104

A large organization with an excellent media presentation. A national conference every year brings together top prolife speakers.

Nurses for Life
P.O. Box 4818
Detroit, MI 48219

They have an extensive organization and an excellent newsletter.

Americans United for Life
230 N. Michigan Ave. #915
Chicago, IL 60601

AUL provides excellent legal and educational resources. Their books include *Abortion and Social Justice; New Perspectives on Human Abortions; Death, Dying and Euthanasia;* and *Infanticide and the Handicapped Newborn.* In addition, AUL staffs four full-time attorneys. They are staff counsel for the AUL Legal Defense Fund, and serve as the legal arm of the prolife movement. The Legal Defense Fund has become a sort of prolife American Civil Liberties Union. Inquiries should be addressed to Mr. Rick Valentine, Executive Director.

The Rutherford Institute
P.O. Box 510
Manassas, VA 22110

Founded by John Whitehead, it specializes in fighting court cases related to religious freedom and prolife causes.

Alternatives to Abortion, International
Suite 511
Hillcrest Hotel
Toledo, OH 43699

AAI grew out of the initiative of Birthright, but acts as an umbrella organization to help pregnant women bring their babies into the world. They also publish an excellent magazine.

Birthright
National Office
"Summerhill"
62 Hunter Street
Woodbury, NJ 08096

This group serves as the premier counseling and care organization. They have over 350 chapters nationwide. Their telephone counselors provide information and help to pregnant women.

Evangelical Adoption and Family Service
201 S. Main Street
North Syracuse, NY 13212

Prospective and Adoptive Parents of America
P.O. Box 138
Glenview, IL 60025

Women Exploited
P.O. Box 57
Homestead, PA 15120

The group was formed by women who have had abortions and believe they were deceived into thinking it was only "a simple, ten-minute operation." Speakers are available.

Books to Read

Bajema, Clifford E. *Abortion and the Meaning of Personhood.* Grand Rapids, MI: Direction Books, 1974.

Brown, Harold O. J. *Death Before Birth.* Nashville, TN: Thomas Nelson, 1977.

Burtchaell, James. *Rachel Weeping and Other Essays on Abortion.* Fairway, KS: Andrews & McMeel, 1982.

Delahoyde, Melinda and Horan, Dennis, J., eds. *Infanticide and the Handicapped Newborn.* Provo, UT: Brigham Young University Press, 1982.

Hensley, Jeff Lane, ed. *The Zero People*. Ann Arbor, MI: Servant Books, 1983.

Hilgers, Thomas W., et al., eds. *New Perspectives on Human Abortion*. Frederick, MD: University Publications, 1981.

―――― and Horan, Dennis J., eds. *Abortion and Social Justice*. Thaxton, VA: Sunlife Books, 1982.

Horan, Dennis J., and Mall, David, eds. *Death, Dying & Euthanasia*. Frederick, MD: University Publications, 1977.

Koop, C. Everett. *The Right to Live; the Right to Die*. Wheaton, IL: Tyndale House, 1976.

Noonan, John T., Jr. *A Private Choice: Abortion in America in the Seventies*. New York: Free Press, 1979.

Schaeffer, Francis A. *A Christian Manifesto*. Westchester, IL.: Crossway Books, 1981.

Schaeffer, Franky. *A Time For Anger*. Westchester, IL: Crossway Books, 1982.

Sobran, Joseph. *Single Issues*. New York: Human Life Press, 1983.

Articles

Alexander, Leo. "Medical Science Under Dictatorship." *New England Journal of Medicine*, 241 (July 1949):39.

Campbell, A. G. M. and Duff, Raymond. "Moral and Ethical Dilemmas in the Special-Care Nursery." *New England Journal of Medicine*, 289 (October 1973):890. Written by two doctors who practiced infanticide in the newborn nursery.

Fletcher, Joseph. "Ethics and Euthanasia." *American Journal of Nursing*, 73 (1973):670. Written by the leading advocate of infanticide and euthanasia.

The leading prolife journal is the *Human Life Review*. This journal provides excellent articles on every aspect of all the life issues. Contributors include the leading medical, legal, and theological scholars on these issues. Anyone wishing to have a comprehensive and current education on abortion, infanticide and euthanasia should read the *Human Life Review* regularly. It is published by the Human Life Foundation, Inc., Room 540, 150 E. 35th Street, New York, NY 10016.

Acknowledgments

First we would like to thank Franky Schaeffer V Productions Inc., most particularly Franky Schaeffer and Jim Buchfuehrer, who worked with us in taking the ideas expressed in this book through every stage of development. Their company financed and arranged for the research and made many direct contributions to the text.

Franky Schaeffer wrote the screenplay for this book's accompanying film series and directed the episodes. Jim Buchfuehrer produced the series. As a team, together they made this project possible.

We want to thank Ray Cioni and the staff of the Cioni Artworks for all their hard work on the film and the hardcover edition of the book.

Another team, the general pediatric surgical staff of the Children's Hospital of Philadelphia and their paramedical personnel, made it possible for one of us to devote the necessary time to complete work on the book and film series.

A number of experts in various fields contributed greatly to the research and development necessary for this project. Professor Kenneth A. Kitchen, lecturer in Egyptian and Coptic at the School of Archaeology and Oriental Studies at the University of Liverpool, England, added much to our knowledge and research for the archaeological data. We had invaluable help from Ranald Macaulay in general research and through his special assistance with chapters 4 and 5.

We want to give special thanks to Melinda Delahoyde, Director of Education, Americans United for Life, for her help in making the revisions to this new edition.

In addition we would thank the following for their contributions: Francis Ackerman, Jerram Barrs, Dr. James B. Hurley, Dr. Jeremy C. Jackson, Dick Keyes, Udo Middelmann, Oliver O'Donovan, John Sandri, and Dr. Joseph Stanton. Their time and efforts are greatly appreciated, as is the editorial work of James W. Sire and Evelyn Sendecke.

Francis A. Schaeffer
C. Everett Koop, M.D.

Notes

[1]The barbarism of the holocaust was not limited to European Jewry. Gypsies, Slavs, Russians, German dissidents for political and religious reasons, resistance leaders from occupied European countries, ordinary captives in the course of war, and even children of some of these former categories were eliminated. However, the Jews were especially slated for total elimination. Heinrich Himmler delivered an address on October 10, 1943, to an assembly of SS generals at Poznan. By this time both Himmler and his audience must have known that Germany could not win the war. Himmler stated: "Among ourselves it should be mentioned quite frankly, and yet we will never speak of it publicly . . . I mean . . . the extirpation of the Jewish race . . . this is a page of glory in our history which has never been written and is never to be written."

[2]The following is the standard form of the Oath of Hippocrates taken by those current medical students who take an oath. This so-called "original" form of the oath is the most widely used, although frequently the reference to Apollo, the Physician, and the other gods is omitted:

I swear by Apollo, the Physician, and Aesculapius and health and all-heal and all the gods and goddesses that, according to my ability and judgment, I will keep this oath and stipulation:
To reckon him who taught me this art equally dear to me as my parents,

to share my substance with him and relieve his necessities if required: to regard his offspring as on the same footing with my own brothers, and to teach them this art if they should wish to learn it, without fee or stipulation, and that by precept, lecture and every other mode of instruction, I will impart a knowledge of the art to my own sons and to those of my teachers, and to disciples bound by a stipulation and oath, according to the law of medicine, but to none others.

I will follow that method of treatment which, according to my ability and judgment, I consider for the benefit of my patients, and abstain from whatever is deleterious and mischievous. I will give no deadly medicine to anyone if asked, nor suggest any such counsel; furthermore, I will not give to a woman an instrument to produce abortion.

With Purity and with Holiness I will pass my life and practice my art. I will not cut a person who is suffering with a stone, but will leave this to be done by practitioners of this work. Into whatever houses I enter I will go into them for the benefit of the sick and will abstain from every voluntary act of mischief and corruption; and further from the seduction of females or males, bond or free.

Whatever, in connection with my professional practice, or not in connection with it, I may see or hear in the lives of men which ought not to be spoken abroad I will not divulge, as reckoning that all such should be kept secret.

While I continue to keep this oath unviolated may it be granted to me to enjoy life and the practice of the art, respected by all men at all times but should I trespass and violate this oath, may the reverse be my lot.

[3]Jaan Kangilaski writing in *Medical Forum* in May 1978 reported on an informal survey of 1977 commencement practices in reference to the Hippocratic Oath. One hundred and thirty-two medical schools were queried; ninety-two responded. Fifty-three schools used the "original" form of the Hippocratic Oath, twenty-six used the Declaration of Geneva, thirteen used the prayer of Maimonides, and seven others used various other pledges, sometimes student written.

Sometimes the oath is administered to the class; sometimes one student or one faculty member recites the pledge and others follow; sometimes the pledge is said by one person while the others stand silent; and at Yale the 1977 program allowed time so that those who wished to take the oath could do so in silence.

[4]George F. Will, *Newsweek,* April 4, 1977, p. 96.

[5]*Time,* August 1, 1977, p. 54.

[6]Edward O. Wilson wrote *Sociobiology: The New Synthesis* in 1975 (Belknap Press of Harvard University). His more recent book (1978)—*On Human Nature* (Harvard University Press)—applies his ideas specifically to human behavior.

[7]*Time,* August 1, 1977, p. 54.

[8]Joan Hutchison, writing in *Challenge* for May/June 1976, started her essay dealing with the history of child abuse in the following way: "Burned, bashed, beaten, stomped, suffocated, strangled, poisoned, choked, ripped, steamed, boiled, dismembered, bitten, raped, clubbed, banged, torn. Ignored, starved, abandoned, exploited, demeaned, ridiculed, treated with coldness and indifference or unreasonable demands."

[9]Gay Pauley, "Of Cries, Whispers, and Incest," *Philadelphia Evening Bulletin,* October 3, 1977.

[10]Gay Pauley, "Incest: Healing Taboos, Harsh Wounds," *Philadelphia Evening Bulletin,* October 4, 1977.

[11]A number of forces at work in America are antifamily. Among these are the constantly climbing divorce rate, the gay-liberation movement, extreme forms of women's lib, and abortion-on-demand. One child in six now lives in a single-parent family. Of every eight women giving birth to a child, one is not married (compared to one in twenty in 1960). More than half of American married women with children of ages six through seventeen are now in the labor force (double the 1948 rate). A third of unmarried women with children under three are in the work force.

[12]Mothers who have had several abortions are more likely than others to beat their children, according to a study conducted by Dr. Burton G. Schoenfeld, a child psychiatrist of Prince Georges County General Hospital in Maryland.

[13]In the National Right to Life *News* of January 1977, Jesse L. Jackson had this to say on the right of privacy: "There are those who argue that the right to privacy is of higher order than the right to life . . . that was the premise of slavery. You could not protest the existence or treatment of slaves on the plantation because that was private and therefore outside your right to be concerned. . . . The Constitution called us three-fifths human and the whites further dehumanized us by calling us 'niggers.' It was part of the dehumanizing process. . . . These advocates taking life prior to birth do not call it killing or murder, they call it abortion. They further never talk about aborting a baby because that would imply something human. . . . Fetus sounds less than human and therefore can be justified. . . .

"What happens to the mind of a person, and the moral fabric of a nation, that accepts the aborting of the life of a baby without a pang of conscience? What kind of a person and what kind of a society will we have twenty years hence if life can be taken so casually? It is that question, the question of our attitude, our value system, and our mind set with regard to the nature and worth of life itself that is the central question confronting mankind. Failure to answer that question affirmatively may leave us with a hell right here on earth."

[14]John T. Noonan, Jr., "Why a Constitutional Amendment?" *Human Life Review* 1:28 (1975).

[15]Ibid.

Did the Court really go so far? Here is what it held:

Until a human being is "viable" or "capable of meaningful life," a state has no "compelling interest" that justifies it in restricting in any way in favor of the fetus a woman's fundamental personal liberty of abortion. For six months, or "usually" for seven months (the Court's reckoning), the fetus is denied the protection of law by virtue of either the Ninth Amendment or the Fourteenth Amendment.

After viability has been reached, the human being is not a person "in the whole sense," so that even after viability he or she is not protected by the Fourteenth Amendment's guarantee that life shall not be taken without due process of law. At this point he or she is, however, legally recognizable as "potential life."

. . . The state may require that after the first trimester abortions be performed in licensed "facilities," and that after viability they be regulated so long as "health" abortions are not denied. The state is constitutionally barred, however, from requiring review of the abortion decision by a hospital committee or concurrence in the decision by two physicians other than the attending physician. The Constitution also prohibits a state from requiring that the abortion be in a hospital licensed by the Joint Committee on Accreditation of Hospitals or indeed that it be in a hospital at all.

[16]Archibald Cox, *The Role of the Supreme Court in American Government* (New York: Oxford University Press, 1976).

[17]It is interesting to note that while over a million unborn babies were being destroyed in the womb each year, the same Supreme Court which made that slaughter possible stopped the construction of the $116,000,000 Tellico Dam in Tennessee—because it might wipe out the snail darter, a three-inch fish. Since then, the threat to the lousewort plant has raised legal questions about building a power plant in Maine, and the orange-bellied mouse has complicated citing requirements for a power plant near San Francisco. A $340,000,000 dam on the Stanislaus River in California ran into legal difficulties because a ⅝-inch daddy-long-legs spider dwells there. There are quotas on whales and porpoises, but it is always open season on unborn babies. Although we can applaud the efforts to preserve our environment, it seems that we have confused our priorities.

[18]The organization Planned Parenthood, on the other hand, is flourishing. With millions and millions of dollars of taxpayers' money (plus substantial sums from private fund raising) and usually working with the American Civil Liberties Union, Planned Parenthood launched an all-out war against pro-life gains. This is a far cry from what its founder Margaret Sanger had in mind when the organization was an active proponent of "birth control." Mrs. Sanger always believed that abortion was killing.

Planned Parenthood-World Population describes itself as "the nation's foremost agent of social change in the area of reproductive health and well-being." In 1976 their audited statement reported $89,900,000 in income. In fact, when Title X funds are considered, Planned Parenthood is fueled with $300,000,000 annually from the United States Government at some level as it pursues its goal.

The law is clear concerning the use of Title X funds for abortion: *None of the funds appropriated under Title X may be used in programs where abortion is a method of family planning.* Planned Parenthood's Jeannie Rosoff contends: "There is no basis for believing that the prohibition of Title X funds for abortion as a method of family planning was intended to prohibit the use of such funds for abortion counseling and referral or even promotion or encouragement of abortion."

[19]Harold O. J. Brown, in comparing the action of the United States Supreme Court with that of the West German Federal Constitutional Court (in an action the latter took in June 1974) had this to say: "The West German Federal Constitutional Court dealt with the question of unlimited right to abortion on demand on the basis of an elevation of fundamental questions concerning the nature of man and the requirements of justice, which the courts held to be reflected in the German Federal Constitution. The decision of the American Court represents the deliberate avoidance of the larger moral, ethical, and anthropological questions to which the German court addressed itself. . . . The comparison between the American and German courts' thinking on the issue was especially disappointing. No one familiar with *Roe* v. *Wade* can fail to recognize that in it the

highest American court has evaded the basic moral issue and resolved a fundamental question only on the basis of technical legal construction." (*see* Harold O. J. Brown, "Abortion: Rights or Technicalities," *Human Life Review*, Vol. 1, No. 3, 1975, pp. 72, 73.)

[20]Harold O. J. Brown, "Abortion and Child Abuse," *Christianity Today*, October 7, 1977, p. 34.

[21]As recently as 1967, at the First International Conference on Abortion, a purely secular group of people said, "We can find no point in time between the union of sperm and egg and the birth of an infant at which point we can say that this is not a human life" (Washington, D.C.: conference sponsored by Harvard Divinity School and Joseph P. Kennedy, Jr., Foundation).

[22]According to nurses' testimony after the uterus was opened at the time of hysterotomy, Dr. Edelin purportedly cut off the blood supply of an allegedly viable fetus by detaching the placenta and waiting three minutes before removing the fetus from the uterus. A number of emotional factors were introduced by the media during this trial. One of these factors was that the trial was taking place in Roman Catholic Boston which obviously should be against abortion. A second of these factors was that Dr. Edelin was black and therefore the trial was seen to be racist. The final conclusion of the case was that a higher court reversed the lower court's decision and Dr. Edelin was not only free but went on to become the president of a national medical organization.

[23]*Markle* v. *Abele* (1972), Supreme Court of the United States, No. 72-56, 72-730, p. 72.

[24]The Waddill case raises a very serious difference between what the Supreme Court has called the woman's right to have an abortion-on-demand and what actually happens in cases of live births following abortion—and that is the destruction of the living baby. There is nothing even implied in the woman's "right" to abortion that says she also has the right to a dead child.

Waddill was charged with strangling a baby girl at Westminster Community Hospital, March 2, 1977, after an unsuccessful abortion attempt. At a preliminary hearing in April 1977 before the jury trial in January 1978, Dr. Ronald Cornelsen testified that Dr. Waddill throttled the infant's neck and complained about what would happen if the baby survived. According to Cornelsen's testimony, Waddill said that there would be lawsuits, that the baby would be brain damaged, and talked about stopping respiration by drowning or injecting potassium chloride.

At the trial in January 1978, Mrs. Joanne Griffith, a nurse at the hospital where the abortion was performed, testified that another nurse had quoted Dr. Waddill on the telephone as ordering everyone involved not to do anything, and to leave the baby alone. Dr. Cornelsen testified at the trial that when he first examined the baby, and the heart was beating sixty to seventy times a minute with a regular rhythm, there was some discoloration on the baby's neck (allegedly from the first attempt at strangling) and further testified that while he was examining the baby, Dr. Waddill ". . . stuck his hand back in [the isolette] and pressed the baby's neck again" (from *The Los Angeles Times*, January 26, February 8, 1978).

Dr. Waddill was brought to trial again on the same charges in the same case in 1979.

[25]*Medical World News*, November 14, 1977.

[26]Ibid.

[27]Ibid.

[28]Ibid.

[29]*Fort Lauderdale News,* November 13, 1977.

[30]Ibid.

[31]"You Be the Judge," *National Newsline,* February 1975 (Dayton, Ohio: Nurses Concerned for Life, Inc.).

[32]Leon Kass, as quoted by George F. Will in "Discretionary Killing," *Newsweek,* September 20, 1976.

[33]The Akron ordinance regulating abortion was put together and guided through City Council by a twenty-three-year-old Orthodox Jew named Marvin Weinberger, a Boston University law student. He took leave from Boston University Law School and formed a group called Citizens for Informed Consent and guided the ordinance from its original draft and early public hearings to a 7-to-6 City Council victory.

[34]Dr. Matthew Bulfin, onetime president of Pro-Life Obstetricians and Gynecologists, has done a study on more than 300 patients who previously had legal abortions and later saw him as gynecological patients. He developed a set of questions that he asked this selected group of patients. Here are some of the things he learned:

The vast majority of women would not have had an abortion if it were illegal to do so.

For 90 percent of the women, a physician apparently never entered into the decision to have an abortion.

The majority of women did not even know the name of the doctor who performed the abortion.

The great majority of patients did not seem to recall any discussion of the risks of the abortion itself or the possible risks of future childbearing.

Not one patient admitted to having any kind of thorough examination until the actual pelvic exam that was done as the abortion was about to be started.

When complications occurred after the abortion, most women reported they did not know the name of the doctor nor had they any confidence in him and therefore usually called their own gynecologist or went to the emergency room of the nearest hospital.

Dr. Bulfin used to ask this question: "Were you aware at any time that you might be destroying a human life when you had your abortion?" The reason he stopped asking the question is that too many patients either broke down in tears or became upset because they thought he might be about to impose a religious prejudice on them (*Newsletter:* Pro-Life Obstetricians and Gynecologists).

[35]It is very difficult to obtain statistics in the United States that illuminate the effects of abortion on the woman. The 1973 Supreme Court ruling, which made possible the establishment of free-standing clinics outside the scrutiny of accreditation groups, contributes to the loss of statistical data for these purposes. The Department of Health, Education and Welfare released an "interim report" in 1978, indicating that women who have had an abortion face an 85 percent higher "spontaneous fetal death ratio" in subsequent pregnancies.

The National Health Service in Great Britain keeps excellent records and has been in the abortion-on-demand business for several years longer than the United States. These records have revealed an increase in illegitimacy, venereal disease, prostitution, and pelvic inflammatory disease from gonorrhea, as well as sterility of previously aborted mothers and subsequent spontaneous abortions or miscarriages. Ectopic pregnancies—where the egg is implanted not in the uterus but in the Fallopian tube, requiring an emergency abdominal operation—have doubled since abortion has been liberalized. Prematurity in British women who have had a previous abortion is 40 percent higher than those who have not.

In May 1976, the *British Medical Journal* reported a paper by Richardson and Dickson entitled "The Effects of Legal Termination on Subsequent Pregnancy" (May 29, 1976, pp. 1303-04). Using the Richardson and Dickson statistics, Barbara J. Siska has done a study on what that means for the one million American woman who abort their babies in a given year (*Newsletter* of National Right to Life Committee, Summer 1976). Projecting from such a small sample as that given by Richardson and Dickson gives only a rough estimate, but close enough to reveal the magnitude of the problems induced by abortion. About 430,000 women who had abortions (out of the 1,000,000) would not now be pregnant a second time had they carried their babies to term, since there would be no time for them to get pregnant. Inasmuch as about 48 percent of all abortions are performed on women who have no living children, Siska had this to say about the 478,000 women (who aborted their first babies): "As many as 88,000 will lose their 'wanted' baby. Taking into account the normal infant mortality rate for 1974 (16.7 per 1,000), 26,000 infants would die solely because their mothers had abortions beforehand."

[36]Harold O. J. Brown has this to say about the separation of church and state: "No American historian would seriously contend that the phrase 'regarding an establishment of religion' in the First Amendment means anything other than what it says: it forbids the establishment of a national religion or church. . . ." (It did not in fact forbid the establishment of *state churches*, as both Massachusetts and Connecticut had them at the time of the amendment's adoption and retained them for many years to come. The limitations of federal power contained in the Bill of Rights have subsequently been extended to apply to the individual states as well. Yet even when applied to the states, the First Amendment means only that no state may establish a state church, just as the federal government may not establish a national church. It certainly did not mean, in its conception, that nothing in public law or policy may reflect the convictions or insights of any church or of the Christian religion [*see* Harold O. J. Brown, "The Passivity of American Christians," *Christianity Today,* January 16, 1976].)

[37]More and more feminists are disgusted with the realities of the abortion situation. One such group is known as Women Exploited. Their leader, Sandra Haun, testified before the Pennsylvania legislature as follows: "The members of our organization have all had abortions and have come to realize, too late, that our decision was wrong. We were encouraged and pushed into a hasty decision that now we find impossible to live with. We were lied to and deliberately misinformed."

[38]From the same Children's Hospital in Sheffield where Robert Zachary works, pediatrician John Lorber, discouraged with the results of surgery on spina bifida (cleft spine) and its complications, has in visits to this country been urging his American counterparts to consider not operating on at least the 20 percent of victims who are severely affected. Lorber claims that among 323 children treated vigorously from 1959 to 1963 only 7 percent were normal.

This view has been countered particularly by Dr. John M. Freeman at Johns

Hopkins University School of Medicine. Freeman quoted a series of 171 patients with spina bifida treated at the University of Pennsylvania between 1963 and 1968. Of the children with thoracolumbar lesions, 42 percent had IQs of 80 or better and were able to get around "albeit often with braces and crutches," said Dr. Freeman, "so the outlook does not have to be as bad as Dr. Lorber would have us believe."

Patients with spina bifida have been frequently reported to die quickly if unattended. This is not so. About 60 percent of untreated patients are alive at a month, 45 percent at two months, 19 percent at one year, and 16 percent at two years. Though these untreated children do not die quickly, they die slowly, over months and years and sometimes don't die at all.

[39]The term *cost containment* is the magic phrase in medical economics today. It did not seem to be the case when the right of every citizen to dialysis, pending kidney transplantation, was established by federal law. But in a few years the cost of intensive care is singled out as being too much for the American people to bear. One is considered an intolerable reactionary if he compares the cost of medical care with that of unnecessary luxuries such as alcohol or tobacco. Nevertheless, the figures invite comparison.

If we are social burdens in days to come, it seems fair to assume that our futures are somewhat limited. If, in addition to being social burdens, we are economic burdens as well, we don't stand a chance.

One is amazed that in the debates concerning the cost of intensive care for premature babies (or youngsters born with congenital defects requiring surgery) so little mention is made of the good news concerning newborn intensive care. The kind of intensive care we are talking about has cut the neonatal death rate in half in less than a generation, and the cost of saving most babies referred to newborn intensive-care units is far less than the figures usually cited for extreme cases. At the Children's Hospital of Philadelphia (where one of us works in neonatal surgery), it would be absolutely impossible to achieve the results that we do in presenting perfectly normal, healthy youngsters to their parents were it not for our absolute dependence upon the technology of intensive care, coupled with the dedication and skill of physicians, nurses, and paramedical personnel.

Jeffrey J. Pomerantz, M.D., of the Cedars-Sinai Medical Center in Los Angeles, studied seventy-five infants weighing less than 1000 grams during the period from 1973 through 1975. He found that thirty infants (40 percent) lived, and 70 percent of these were judged to be neurologically and developmentally normal (one to three years later). Thus the intact survival rate was 28 percent.

Pomerantz calculated the average daily cost for each survivor to be $450. By dividing the total cost for all the babies by the twenty-one intact survivors, he found an average cost per "normal" survivor of $88,058. Even with inflation adjustment, Pomerantz concluded, "It is our belief, that the outcome justifies this expense" (*Pediatrics,* June 1978, as reported in *American Medical News*).

[40]A study was done in 1977 on the impact of an abnormal child upon the parents. In summary, thirty families with a newborn mongoloid baby were matched with thirty families with a normal baby. Both groups were followed for eighteen months to two years and interviewed six times. Few differences could be found in the mental or physical health of the parents in the two groups.

Interestingly enough, a low rate of broken homes was found among the families of mongoloid children living at home. There was an increased incidence of divorce and separation in families of similar children in institutions.

Author Ann Gath reports, "Despite their grief, the parents of almost half the mongol children in the study felt drawn closer together and their marriage rather strengthened than weakened by their shared tragedy, a view similar to that expressed by parents of older mongol children in a survey of school age siblings of mongol children [done earlier]" (*British Journal of Psychiatry*, 1977, 130:405-10).

A study by Burton in 1975 revealed that 64 percent of mothers and 53 percent of fathers of children with fibrocystic disease also believed that their problems and distress had brought them closer to their spouses. (*See* L. Burton, *The Family Life of Sick Children*, London: Routledge and Keagan, 1975).

[41]One of the most remarkable medical achievements in the world today is to be found centered in the Parisian suburb of Garches. Here, after acute care at the Raymond Poincare Hospital, a private paramedical corporation is overseeing the care of 450 patients on respirators in their own homes. Some of these patients are on total respiratory support, others only on demand. Many have completed their higher education and some are employed in responsible consultant positions. It is a marvelous example of hospital personnel, paramedical technicians, the government's assisting private enterprise, and the will of individuals to succeed in spite of handicaps. The man whose vision this was is a paraplegic.

[42]Another factor that must always be considered in such cases, although one does not plan them that way, is that what is learned in one individual spectacular success eventually has benefit to untold thousands of subsequent patients.

About a decade ago we had a newborn patient whose entire small bowel was gangrenous, and in desperation one of our surgeons put the bowel together after removing the gangrenous portion in the only possible way—but one which was incompatible with eventual survival. It was on this diminutive patient that the first total parenteral (other than intestinal) nutritional program ever tried on an infant was carried out. Although that youngster tragically succumbed to sepsis well over a year after her initial operation, the knowledge gained in that instance has benefitted literally thousands upon thousands of children the world over, to say nothing of the adults who have benefitted as well. Total parenteral nutrition as worked out on this youngster is perhaps one of the four or five outstanding medical achievements of the past decade.

[43]A questionnaire mailed to members of the surgical section of the American Academy of Pediatrics in 1975 sought to explore the beliefs and practices of the surgical Fellows concerning ethical issues in the care of the newborn with a life-threatening defect which was correctable by a surgical procedure.

While acknowledging the difficulties inherent in interpreting a questionnaire, it was clear that a substantial number of this group of elite surgeons would acquiesce to parents' wishes in not treating a newborn, but rather allowing him or her to die with intestinal atresia (obstruction with excellent prognosis after operation) alone (7.9 percent) or accompanied by mongolism (76.8 percent).

[44]Millard Everett, *Ideals of Life: An Introduction to Ethics and the Humanities, With Readings* (New York: Wiley, 1954). *Note:* This was quoted in *The Way We Die* by David Dempsey.

[45]In response to the publication of "Moral and Ethical Dilemmas in the Special-

Care Nursery" in the *New England Journal of Medicine* by Duff and Campbell in October of 1973, there appeared among other letters to the editor in the same journal (February 28, 1974) one by Joan L. Venes, M.D., and Peter R. Huttenlocher, M.D., of the Yale University School of Medicine. They described themselves as some of the "specialists based in the medical center" referred to by Duff and Campbell. This is the final paragraph of that letter:

"As consultants to the Newborn Special Care Unit, we wish to dissociate ourselves from the opinions expressed by the authors. The 'growing tendency to seek early death as a management option' that the authors referred to has been repeatedly called to the attention of those involved and has caused us deep concern. It is troubling to us to hear young pediatric interns ask first, 'Should we treat?' rather than 'How do we treat?': we are fearful that this feeling of nihilism may not remain restricted to the Newborn Special Care Unit. To suggest that the financial and psychological stresses imposed upon a family with the birth of a handicapped child constitutes sufficient justification for such a therapy of nihilism is untenable and allows us to escape what perhaps after all are the real issues—i.e., the obligation of an affluent society to provide financial support and the opportunity for a gainful life to its less fortunate citizens."

[46]Here is a quotation from a pediatric surgeon, appended to a questionnaire on his attitude toward patients with Down's syndrome: "I have a fifty-three-year-old cousin with Down's syndrome. His father is a ninety-three-year-old arteriosclerotic, incontinent at night of urine and stool. He refuses to go to a nursing home. They live alone and the son with Down's syndrome provides most of the care."

[47]Anthony Shaw, "Dilemmas of Informed Consent in Children," *New England Journal of Medicine,* October 25, 1973, pp. 885-890.

[48]*The Hastings Center Report,* Vol. 2, No. 5 (November 1972).

[49]"Euthanasia and Children: The Injury of Continued Existence," *Journal of Pediatrics,* 83 (1973), pp. 170, 171.

[50]J. Philip Wogaman in *The Washington Post,* August 16, 1977.

[51]*The New York Times,* July 28, 1977.

[52]*Commentary,* 53:8 (May 1972).

[53]Martha Willing, *Beyond Conception: Our Children's Children* (Ipswich, Massachusetts: Gambit, 1971), p. 174.

[54]*Medical Tribune,* July 20, 1977, pp. 23, 29.

[55]This book was probably the beginning of the German rationale for what began as euthanasia programs and ended up as attempted genocide of specific groups.

[56]The Quinlan case should never have gone to court in the first place. The medical malpractice climate in the United States at the time (and still present) was probably the major factor which initiated the court proceeding. Many in the medical profession hailed the decision on the part of the Quinlans to go to court, when they should have been appalled at the implications for their own future practice of medicine.

What the Karen Quinlan case threatened was the disruption of the patient-family-doctor relationship. It foretold the day when the doctor would become a technical instrument in the hands of the court and a hospital ethics committee.

Richard A. McCormick, S.J., of the Kennedy Institute Center for Bioethics in Washington, D.C., said it very well this way: ". . . the abiding issue [in the Quinlan case] is . . . the very moral matrix of the healing profession. That matrix roots in the conviction that decision making within health care . . . must be controlled primarily within the patient-doctor-family relationship and these decisions must be tailor made to individual cases and circumstances. If technology and law were largely to usurp these prerogatives . . . impersonal consideration would replace personal ones and preprogram our treatment. . . ."

[57]The New Jersey Supreme Court overruled the lower court in a 7-0 decision on March 31, 1976. The decision was as follows: "Upon the concurrence of the guardian [the father] and family of Karen, should the responsible attending physicians conclude that there is no reasonable possibility of Karen's ever emerging from her present comatose condition in a cognitive sapient state and that the self-support apparatus now being administered to Karen should be discontinued, they shall consult with the hospital's 'ethics committee' or like body of the institution in which Karen is then hospitalized.

"If that consultative body agrees . . . the present life support system may be withdrawn and said action shall be without any civil or criminal liability therefore on the part of any participant, whether guardian, physician, hospital or others. . . ."

So the ethics committee was written into the decision. Dr. Karen Teel (*Baylor Law Review* 6:8-9, 1975) stated that many hospitals have an ethics committee made up not only of physicians but also social workers, attorneys, and theologians. In a report in the *Medical Tribune* (January 5, 1977) Dr. Teel later said, "I now have more and more reservations concerning the establishment of ethics committees. . . . I now believe that each case must be decided on its own merits."

[58]The United States Supreme Court had refused to be drawn into the Karen Quinlan case in its refusal to review the decision of the New Jersey Supreme Court. At the time of this writing, February 1979, Karen is still alive.

[59]Since the Karen Quinlan case, medical and other literature has been filled with "guidelines" for the physician in difficult situations. But see how easily guidelines for stopping life-prolonging treatments for dying or comatose patients (which is commonly practiced by reputable physicians all over the world) can readily be turned into directives for euthanasia. A perfect example is when the Swiss Academy of Medical Sciences issued such guidelines. As reported in *The New York Times* with a dateline of Basel, Switzerland: "A doctor said if the 'directives concerning euthanasia were applied in the United States, doctors would be permitted to end intravenous feedings of Karen Quinlan, the comatose New Jersey woman whose case set off an international debate.' " There are a number of misconceptions in this Swiss doctor's statement. First of all, the directives given by the Swiss Academy of Medical Sciences were not euthanasia guidelines, but he saw fit immediately to use that term as being synonymous with the Academy's statement. Second, Karen Quinlan is not being fed by intravenous feedings, but by feedings introduced via a nasogastric tube. We call attention to this difference because improper reporting in this instance could legitimately raise the question of whether feedings by tube were as "extraordinary" as intravenous feedings in the care of Karen Quinlan.

[60]Robert R. Durzon, administrator of HEW's new health-care financing administration, suggested in a memorandum to Joseph A. Califano, secretary of HEW, in June of 1977 that federal Medicare funds be withheld from states that do not enact living-will laws which permit terminally ill patients to have life-support

equipment withdrawn. The memorandum stated: "Encouraging states to pass such a law or, more strongly, withholding federal funds without passage would lower health spending when such wills are executed. . . . Over one-fifth of Medicare expenditures are for persons in their last year of life. Thus in fiscal year 1978, $4.9 billion dollars will be spent for such persons and if just one-quarter of these expenditures were avoided through adoption of living wills, the savings under Medicare alone would amount to $1.2 billion . . ." (reported Wednesday, June 22, 1977, in the *Washington Post*).

[61] An example of such a board's going beyond its proscribed boundaries by natural progression is found in the Human Rights Commission's assumption of abortion as one of its arenas of activity.

[62] *Medical Tribune,* October 10, 1973.

[63] Joseph Fletcher, "Ethics and Euthanasia," *American Journal of Nursing,* 73:670 (1973).

[64] Medically, Fletcher's example is not a good one. It is possible to have brain metastases revealed by a brain scan and not be in either pain or extremis.

[65] *Philadelphia Evening Bulletin,* August 13, 1977.

[66] *Time,* September 5, 1977, p. 29.

[67] *Philadelphia Evening Bulletin,* August 13, 1977.

[68] *Newsweek,* July 4, 1977.

[69] Richard L. Rubenstein, *The Cunning of History: Mass Death and the American Future* (New York: Harper & Row, 1975).

[70] Frederic Wertham in *A Sign for Cain: An Exploration of Human Violence* (New York: Macmillan, 1966, 1969) makes it quite clear that people of various classes in Germany surrendered their own individual will and conscience to that of the state. The dehumanization and depersonalization which followed in Germany—and this is the lesson for us—was not that the German people and the Nazis in particular were ideologically fanatical with hatred for their victims, but rather they were totally indifferent to their fate.

Those who carried out the killings in the euthanasia programs were academic physicians, many times professors in outstanding universities. They were not "mad" in the sense that we talk about mad scientists; they had fallen under the spell of utilitarianism and were more concerned about the cost of caring for a patient as opposed to killing him.

[71] Leo Alexander, "Medical Science Under Dictatorship," *New England Journal of Medicine,* 241:39–47, July 14, 1949. (This was also covered in *Newsweek,* July 9, 1973.)

[72] Ibid.

[73] Ibid.

[74] We believe that the "living will" will be one of the actual instruments which act as the *thin edge of the wedge* in opening up our society to the euthanasia movement. The living will is a document (now enacted as law in several of the states) which directs physicians concerning the maker's terminal illness and extraordinary care.

The first major stumbling block in any living will centers around the use of the word *terminal* when it refers to the patient's illness. The living will gives to the physician certain rights which might not be the intent of the patient, who may not know that his illness is terminal and/or whose death might not be imminent.

It is very difficult to say when death is imminent. The first patient for whom one of us [C. E. Koop] would have ever been able to sign an affadavit in reference to the imminence of death had what was thought to be a *terminal* neuroblastoma. The patient has graduated from law school and is alive more than thirty years later. This experience has been repeated time after time. In the language of the California Act, it is the physician's decision which makes death "imminent."

In the Arkansas legislation, Section 1 includes the terms *artificial, extraordinary, extreme* or *radical,* and *medical or surgical means or procedures* in the case of a patient unable to discuss this matter with his physician. Even a layman could see that this opens Pandora's box.

75Dr. Richard M. Hunt, "No Fault Guilt-Free History," *The New York Times,* February 16, 1976. Copyright © 1976 by The New York Times Company. Used by permission.

76Donald P. Warwich, "The Moral Message of Bucharest," *The Hastings Center Report,* December 19, 1974.

77One can say things accurately but obscurely, so that the true meaning is present but hidden. A fertilized egg is a zygote. Who would suspect that a postcoital antizygotic pill would prevent the implantation of the fertilized egg?

In 1965 the American College of Obstetricians and Gynecologists changed the definition of human pregnancy. Conception ceased to mean "fertilization"; conception thereafter meant "implantation."

In the American College of Gynecology Terminology *Bulletin* (September 1965) conception is redefined as the implantation of a fertilized ovum. "This definition has been selected deliberately because union of sperm and ovum cannot be detected clinically unless implantation occurs."

78"When Scientists Play the Role of God," *London Times,* November 16, 1978.

79H. J. Blackham, et al., *Objections to Humanism* (Riverside, Connecticut: Greenwood Press, 1967).

80We would like to include a word about rationalism. The Enlightenment was a revolution in thought which took place in the eighteenth century in Europe. One of its main ideas was that man is autonomous; that is, man starts out from himself and measures all things by himself. Thus, there was no place for revelation. The philosophers felt that *reason* (man's) should be supreme, rather than any communication from God.

Looked at from this viewpoint, this movement is called rationalism. This word means that its proponents assumed that man (though finite and limited) can begin from himself and gather all the information needed to explain all things. Rationalism rejects knowledge outside of man himself, especially any knowledge from God. Rationalism led naturally to the present predominant world view we have described at the beginning of this chapter: that is, *materialism* (only matter exists) or *naturalism* (no supernatural exists).

Having this as their world view, the rationalists had increasingly no place for things which were said to be "supernatural," such as miracles, the raising of the dead, and Christ's Transfiguration. These things were, therefore, first said to be beyond knowledge and thus of little or no value. Later they were arbitrarily said to be impossible. This view did not come because of scientific facts, but was rooted in the rationalist world view which they accepted.

Influenced by this thinking, the philosophers and rationalistic theologians made a division in the Bible between those things which fitted in with their rationalistic ideas and those which did not. Their attitude can be summed up simply: God cannot be known as One who acts in history. Therefore, they tried to divide the Bible roughly into natural and supernatural parts. They felt that the supernatural parts were unworthy to be accepted by "modern man," that they belonged necessarily to the realm of primitive superstition, that there was nothing objectively true about them.

An example of one who took this approach is the German scholar David Friedrich Strauss who wrote *The Life of Jesus* in 1835. In it he said that most of the material in the Gospels is "mythical." Speaking of the Transfiguration, he wrote, "It is impossible to maintain this historical, supernatural interpretation which the New Testament sanctions." So what he proposed was a thoroughgoing demythologizing of the Gospel story. The real history, he said, had to be separated from this mythology.

Strauss was not the first scholar to state such opinions, but you can see from the date of *The Life of Jesus*—1835—that the revolution took place a long time ago. The movement as a whole has been called "religious liberalism," because of its "free" approach to the Bible. It grew in momentum during the nineteenth century, and its assumptions are still the assumptions of many scholars in the Protestant world today and of an increasing number of Roman Catholic theologians, too.

What is most disturbing about this approach to the Bible is not that it disagrees with past traditions, but rather that it claims to be "scientific." We must be clear that Christianity has nothing to fear from modern science. Indeed, Christianity was instrumental in the origin of science. Tradition and authority should not be just blindly accepted, but examined to see if the things previously believed are indeed true. What *is* dangerous is the misuse of the claim to be "scientific." We do not think it is too strong to speak of this as "deception."

By using the word *scientific,* the religious liberalists gave the impression of the same type of certainty and objectivity that had become accepted in regard to the physical sciences. Using this claim, they proposed their various theories of how the Bible had actually come into existence, and on the basis of these theories altered the teaching that Christians had previously accepted. They rejected the Bible's accounts of miracles, such as the feeding of the 5,000 or Jesus' walking on the water. But they went much further than that. For example, they rejected the idea of a coming judgment for mankind, of salvation through the substitutionary work of Christ, of the divinity of Christ, of the Resurrection, of the Virgin Birth, and so on. What was left was a religion of morality, called by some the "Religion of the Sermon on the Mount" (though this itself was a serious misrepresentation, for the Sermon on the Mount, as well as teaching a very high moral code, also teaches quite explicitly such things as future judgment by Jesus Himself).

To ordinary people, these developments were bewildering. However, for many the radical conclusions of the scholars seemed to be irresistible, for they were presented as the result of careful and objective scientific scholarship. To disagree with the scholars was to be obscurantist. To maintain the traditional ideas simply indicated a refusal to follow the truth wherever the truth led.

From where we stand today, it is easy to see how naive these views really are.

For what has happened since that time is, first, that the internal weaknesses of the so-called scientific theories have become apparent. Second, literally tons of archaeological materials have been unearthed from the periods and the geographic locations covered by the Bible. Archaeology as a science has made huge strides in the last hundred years.

The scholars fail at this point because they are not scientific enough! They have fallen into the same trap which they accuse those who preceded them of falling into—of bringing preconceived ideas about God's revelation to bear on the discipline of biblical criticism. Because of their world view they refuse to accept the possibility that God could have communicated to man in such a way that what is contained in the Bible is reliable. They caricature this idea with such terms as the "dictation theory of inspiration." By this they act as though the scholars through the centuries (who have held that God has given us truth through the Bible) have taught (and must teach) that God used the human writers of the Bible like typewriters, simply typing out what He wanted man to understand. But, while some may have taught the dictation theory of inspiration, it was not the generally held concept.

The generally held concept was that God used people in the writing of the Bible without destroying their individuality and their significance. What they finally wrote, however, was what God knew was necessary for people to have as a written authority. Each writer was "himself," so to speak, but as each wrote—in a different style from others, in a different historical context, in different literary forms, and sometimes in different languages—he was led by God to write what God intended to be written. Thus, truth was given in all the areas the Bible touches upon.

The critics have continued the tradition received from the last century, which argued that God could not work into the world supernaturally. As Strauss said, "It is *impossible* to maintain as historical the supernatural interpretations the New Testament sanctions." Strauss was correct on one point here. What the New Testament (including the teaching of Christ) teaches about the supernatural happenings in observable history is exactly what Strauss and the other liberal theologians have denied.

It is this sort of thinking which still underlies so much liberal scholarship. Why is it impossible, for example, for God to have effected the Virgin Birth when Jesus was born? After all, since God designed the birth process in the first place, why can He not in one case interrupt the normal action of cause and effect that He created and initiate something different? In the same way, if God created everything at the beginning, why can He not also give life to the dead and raise up Jesus' body from the tomb? The only reason these things and others like them are so categorically denied is that the rationalist or naturalist world view has already been accepted.

When you hear people being critical about the Bible, remember that what seems to be scientific is not always so, and what are claimed to be the "assured results of scholarship" are not always so assured.

Let us give a recent example relating to the dating of the New Testament documents. For over a hundred years the idea has circulated among many scholars that the documents of the New Testament (or most of them) could not have been written at, or soon after, the time of Jesus' ministry. These scholars suggested in some cases that the Gospels were written about 150 years later and were therefore quite unreliable. In the same way, it was common for scholars to suggest that letters supposedly written by Paul or Peter or John were not written by them but by unknown writers who used the apostles' names many years after they died to gain acceptance for what they had written.

A New Testament scholar, the ex-Bishop of Woolwich, John Robinson, now dean of Trinity College, Cambridge, has written a book called *Redating the New Testament* (1976). What is striking is that previously this author had taken a very "liberal" position. At the outset of his book on the dating of the New Testament, he says he first began to question the late dates assigned to the New Testament writers when he realized how "much more than is generally recognised, the chronology of the New Testament rests upon presuppositions rather than facts." And he quotes the following from a letter from a famous New Testament scholar, C. H. Dodd: "I should agree with you that much of this late dating is quite arbitrary, even wanton, the offspring not of any argument that can be presented."

[81]Francis Bacon, *The New Organon and Related Writings* (Indianapolis: Bobbs-Merrill, 1960).

[82]René Descartes, *Meditations on First Philosophy* (Indianapolis: Bobbs-Merrill, 1960).

[83]H. J. Blackham, et al., *Objections to Humanism* (Riverside, Connecticut: Greenwood Press, 1967).

[84]Ibid.

[85]David Hume, *A Treatise of Human Nature* (New York: E. P. Dutton, 1956).

[86]Steven Weinberg, *The First Three Minutes: A Modern View of the Origin of the Universe* (New York: Basic Books, 1976).

[87]Aldous Huxley, *Brave New World* (New York: Harper & Row, 1932).

[88]Robert M. Pirsig, *Zen and the Art of Motorcycle Maintenance: An Inquiry Into Values* (New York: William Morrow, 1974).

[89]Two important arguments for Charles Darwin (1809-1882) and those he convinced have now been almost totally abandoned by evolutionists. The first involves vestigial organs, which (it was supposed) had served useful functions in an earlier stage of man's evolutionary development, but which later became literally useless by the changes brought about through natural selection. Vestigial organs are like crutches one uses after being injured in an accident. They serve a purpose for a time, but when the leg is better the crutches are no longer needed. Certain organs were said to be "vestiges," that is, leftovers from a previous stage in evolution. The simple problem with the argument is that as medical science has developed, most of these organs have been found to serve useful functions in the body.

A second important argument for Darwin and those he convinced is the dictum that "ontogeny recapitulates phylogeny." This idea is that the human embryo goes through the stages of evolution inside the mother's womb, resembling at one stage the fish and so on. The better we understand the embryo, however, the more dubious this argument is seen to be.

Yet, even if these two arguments have been largely given up, many still place their faith in the theory of an unbroken line from the molecule to man by chance. However, they are faced in modern discussions with at least two problems. First, the more fossil evidence we find, the more apparent it becomes that there have always been distinct breaks in the fossil record. Darwin admitted that the paleontological evidence in his day was slender, but, he said, as more is discovered the new evidence will support the hypothesis. This just has not happened.

The evidence of preman is sketchy, and recent discoveries in Africa and elsewhere have generated some difficult new problems in this area. But it is not just the so-called missing links between man and preman that constitute the problem, but *all* the missing links, right down the whole line. Not only are links missing; the chains themselves are missing. If one removes the speculative guesses, rather than links of different chains leading from simple to more complex organisms, one finds virtual explosions of mature life forms at different periods in geological time and many simple forms of life that remain unchanged for several millions of years up to their extinction or even to today.

The second major difficulty for today's evolutionist is that there is no sufficient mechanism to explain how lower life forms can be transformed into higher ones, no matter how much time is allowed. Natural selection cannot bear this weight. Current genetic theories seem even to point to natural selection as working *against* the direction of evolution. Despite the unlikely possibility of mutations that are advantageous, natural selection seems to simplify the genetic endowment of any group rather than lead it to higher orders of complexity.

[90] Pierre Teilhard de Chardin (1881-1955) is an example of this. He was a member of the Jesuit order and a French paleontologist and philosopher. His approach to evolution was an attempt to solve these problems through the use of mystical language, which did justice to neither clear Christian teaching nor scientific thought.

[91] Paul Hazard, *European Thought in the Eighteenth Century: From Montesquieu to Lessing* (Magnolia, Massachusetts: Peter Smith).

[92] Albert Camus, *The Myth of Sisyphus and Other Essays* (New York: Alfred A. Knopf, 1955).

[93] William Barrett, *Irrational Man: A Study in Existential Philosophy* (New York: Doubleday, 1958), p. 248.

[94] The site of the biblical city called Lachish is about thirty miles southwest of Jerusalem. This city is referred to on a number of occasions in the Old Testament. Imagine a busy city with high walls surrounding it, and a gate in front that is the only entrance to the city. We know so much about Lachish from archaeological studies that a reconstruction of the whole city has been made in detail. This can be seen at the British Museum in the Lachish Room in the Assyrian section.

There is also a picture made by artists in the eighth century before Christ, the Lachish Relief, which was discovered in the city of Nineveh in ancient Assyria. In this picture we can see the Jewish inhabitants of Lachish surrendering to Sennacherib, the king of Assyria. The details in the picture and the Assyrian writing on it give the Assyrian side of what the Bible tells us in Second Kings:

> In the fourteenth year of King Hezekiah's reign, Sennacherib king of Assyria attacked all the fortified cities of Judah and captured them. So Hezekiah king of Judah sent this message to the king of Assyria at Lachish: "I have done wrong. Withdraw from me, and I will pay whatever you demand of me." The king of Assyria exacted from Hezekiah king of Judah three hundred talents of silver and thirty talents of gold. So Hezekiah gave him all

the silver that was found in the temple of the LORD and in the treasuries of the royal palace.

At this time Hezekiah king of Judah stripped off the gold with which he had covered the doors and doorposts of the temple of the LORD, and gave it to the king of Assyria.

2 Kings 18:13-16

We should notice two things about this. First, this is a real-life situation—a real siege of a real city with real people on both sides of the war—and it happened at a particular date in history, near the turn of the eighth century B.C. Second, the two accounts of this incident in 701 B.C. (the account from the Bible and the Assyrian account from Nineveh) do not contradict, but rather confirm each other. The history of Lachish itself is not so important for us, but it does illustrate how the Bible can be, and is, confirmed historically even in some of its smaller historical details.

A much more dramatic story surrounds the discovery of the Dead Sea Scrolls in the present century. The Dead Sea Scrolls, some of which relate to the text of the Bible, were found at Qumran, about fifteen miles from Jerusalem.

Most of the Old Testament was originally written in Hebrew, and the New Testament in Greek. Many people have been troubled by the length of time that has elapsed between the original writing of the documents and the present translations. How could the originals be copied from generation to generation and not be grossly distorted in the process? There is, however, much to reassure confidence in the texts we have.

In the case of the New Testament, there are codes of the whole New Testament (that is, manuscripts in book form, like the Codes Sinaiticus and Codex Alexandrinus, dated around the fourth and fifth centuries respectively) and also thousands of fragments, some of them dating back to the second century. The earliest known so far is kept in the John Rylands Library in Manchester, England. It is only a small fragment, containing on one side John 18:31-33 and on the reverse, verses 37 and 38. It is important, however, both for its early date (about A.D. 125) and for the place where it was discovered, namely Egypt. This shows that John's Gospel was known and read in Egypt at that early time. There are thousands of such New Testament texts in Greek from the early centuries after Christ's death and resurrection.

In the case of the Old Testament, however, there was once a problem. There were no copies of the Hebrew Old Testament in existence which dated from before the ninth century after Christ. This did not mean that there was no way to check the Old Testament, for there were other translations in existence, such as the Syriac and the Septuagint (a translation into Greek from several centuries before Christ). However, there was no *Hebrew* version of the Old Testament from earlier than the ninth century after Christ—because to the Jews the Scripture was so holy it was the common practice to destroy the copies of the Old Testament when they wore out, so that they would not fall into any disrespectful use.

Then, in 1947, a Bedouin Arab made a discovery not far from Qumran, which changed everything. While looking for sheep, he came across a cave in which he discovered some earthenware jars containing a number of scrolls. (These jars are now in the Israeli Shrine of the Book in Jerusalem.) Since that time at least ten other caves in the same vicinity have yielded up other scrolls and fragments. Copies of all the Old Testament books except Esther have been discovered (in part or complete) among these remains. One of the most dramatic single pieces was a copy of the Book of Isaiah dated approximately a hundred years before Christ. What was particularly striking about this is the great closeness of the discovered text to the Hebrew text, which we previously had, a text written about a thousand years later!

On the issue of text, the Bible is unique as ancient documents go. No other book from that long ago exists in even a small percentage of the copies we have of the Greek and Hebrew texts which make up the Bible. We can be satisfied that we have a copy in our hands which closely approximates the original. Of course, there have been some mistakes in copying, and all translations lose something of the original language. That is inevitable. But the fact that most of us use translations into French, German, Chinese, English, and so on does not mean that we have an inadequate idea of what was written originally. We lose some of the nuances of the language, even when the translation is good, but we do not lose the essential content and communication.

We looked earlier at the city of Lachish. Let us return to the same period in Israel's history when Lachish was besieged and captured by the Assyrian King Sennacherib. The king of Judah at that time was Hezekiah.

Perhaps you remember the story of how Jesus healed a blind man and told him to go and wash in the Pool of Siloam. It is the same place known by King Hezekiah, approximately 700 years earlier. One of the remarkable things about the flow of the Bible is that historical events separated by hundreds of years took place in the same geographic spots and, standing in these places today, we can feel that flow of history about us. The crucial archaeological discovery which relates to the Pool of Siloam is the tunnel which lies behind it.

One day in 1880 a small Arab boy was playing with his friend and fell into the pool. When he clambered out, he found a small opening about two feet wide and five feet high. On examination, it turned out to be a tunnel reaching back into the rock. But that was not all. On the side of the tunnel an inscribed stone (now kept in the museum in Istanbul) was discovered, which told how the tunnel had been built originally. The inscription in classical Hebrew reads as follows:

> The boring through is completed. And this is the story of the boring: while yet they plied the pick, each toward his fellow, and while there were yet three cubits [4¼ feet] to be bored through, there was heard the voice of one calling to the other that there was a hole in the rock on the right hand and on the left hand. And on the day of the boring through the workers on the tunnel struck each to meet his fellow, pick upon pick. Then the water poured from the source to the Pool 1,200 cubits [about 600 yards] and a 100 cubits was the height of the rock above the heads of the workers in the tunnel.

We know this as Hezekiah's Tunnel. The Bible tells us how Hezekiah made provision for a better water supply to the city: "As for the other events of Hezekiah's reign, all his achievements and how he made the pool and the tunnel by which he brought water into the city, are they not written in the book of the annals of the kings of Judah?" (2 Kings 20:20). We know here three things: the biblical account, the tunnel itself of which the Bible speaks, and the original stone with its inscription in classical Hebrew.

From the Assyrian side, there is additional confirmation of the incidents mentioned in the Bible. There is a clay prism in the British Museum called the Taylor Prism (British Museum, Ref. 91032). It is only fifteen inches high and was discovered in the Assyrian palace at Nineveh. This particular prism dates from about 691 B.C. and tells about Sennacherib's exploits. A section from the prism reads, "As for Hezekiah, the Jew, who did not submit to my yoke, forty-six of his strong walled cities, as well as small cities in their neighbourhood I have besieged and took . . . himself like a caged bird, I shut up in Jerusalem, his royal city. Earthworks I threw up against him." Thus, there is a three-way confirmation concerning Hezekiah's tunnel from the Hebrew side and this amazing confirmation from the Assyrian side.

There is also a confirmation of what the Bible says concerning the Egyptian King Tirhakah who came up to oppose the Assyrians. Confirmation of his reality is typified by a sphinx-ram in the British Museum (British Museum, Ref. B.B. 1779). The small figure between the legs of the ram is a representation of King Tirhakah. The Bible says that when Sennacherib heard that Tirhakah, king of Egypt, was coming to fight against him, he sent messengers to tell Hezekiah that help from Egypt would be of no use to him (see 2 Kings 19:9, 10 and Isaiah 37:9, 10).

The date of Sennacherib's campaign in Palestine is 701 B.C., and something which has often puzzled historians is the role of Tirhakah, who was not king of Egypt and Ethiopia until 690 B.C. But the solution to this problem is simple. In 701 B.C. Tirhakah was only a prince at the side of his military brother, the new Pharaoh Shebitku, who sent Tirhakah with an army to help Hezekiah fend off the Assyrian advance. But the story in Kings and Isaiah does not end in 701 B.C. It carries right through to the death of Sennacherib in 681 B.C., which is nine years after Tirhakah had become king of Egypt and Ethiopia. In other words, the biblical narrative, from the standpoint of 681 B.C., mentions Tirhakah by the title he bore at that time (that is, 681 B.C.), not as he was in 701 B.C. This is still done today, using a man's title as he is known at the time of writing even if one is speaking of a previous time in his personal history.

Unaware of the importance of these facts, and falling into wrong interpretations of some of Tirhakah's inscriptions, some Old Testament scholars have stumbled over each other in their eagerness to diagnose historical errors in the Books of Kings and Isaiah. But as the archaeological confirmation shows, they were quite mistaken. What is striking about these archaeological finds is the way they often converge; there is often not just one line of evidence but several in which the biblical account is confirmed. We do not have confirmation of every single detail in the biblical account, by any means. Nor do we need such total confirmation in view of the amount of evidence there is. To insist on confirmation at every point would be to treat the Bible in a prejudiced way, simply because it is the Bible. The fact that it is a religious book does not mean that it cannot also be true when it deals with history.

Not all archaeological finds have a convergence of many different interrelated lines like these around the life of Hezekiah, but they are no less striking. For example, take the "ration tablets" discovered in the ruins of Babylon. The Bible tells us that after the Assyrians had destroyed the northern kingdom of Samaria (around 721 B.C.), the southern kingdom, Judah, survived for almost another 150 years until approximately 586 B.C. By this time Assyria, one of the greatest military powers of the ancient world, had been defeated by Babylon, a neighboring state to the east. That was in 609 B.C. Four years later the Babylonian general, Nebuchadnezzar—then the crown prince—came west and completely defeated Necho II, king of Egypt, at the battle of Carchemish. As a result of this victory he laid claim to Judah, which had previously been within the sphere of influence of Egypt. King Jehoiakim of Judah thus now paid tribute to the Babylonians. The Bible tells us that Jehoiakim rebelled three years later: "During Jehoiakim's reign, Nebuchadnezzar king of Babylon invaded the land, and Jehoiakim became his vassal for three years. But then he changed his mind and rebelled against Nebuchadnezzar" (2 Kings 24:1).

The political background for this step can be understood from the Babylonian Chronicles (British Museum, Ref. 21946, records events from 597 B.C. down to 594). These were a compressed chronological summary of the principal events from the Babylonian court. There had been a crucial battle in 601 B.C. between the Egyptians and the Babylonians. This had left both sides weakened, and Jehoiakim took this opportunity to declare his independence of the Babylonian king. His independence, or rather Judah's independence, did not last long, for Jehoiakim himself died in 598 B.C., leaving his throne and the crisis to his son, Jehoiachin. Second Kings tells us what happened:

> At that time the officers of Nebuchadnezzar king of Babylon advanced on Jerusalem and laid siege to it, and Nebuchadnezzar himself came up to the city. . . . Jehoiachin king of Judah, his mother, his attendants, his nobles and his officials all surrendered to him.
> In the eighth year of the reign of the king of Babylon, he took Jehoiachin prisoner. . . . He made Mattaniah, Jehoiachin's uncle, king in his place and changed his name to Zedekiah.
>
> 2 Kings 24:10-12, 17

The story of Jehoiachin does not end there, however. The royal family were kept at the court of Nebuchadnezzar, and the Bible says that they, like other royal captives, were provided for by the king with rations of grain and oil:

> In the thirty-seventh year of the exile of Jehoiachin king of Judah, in the year Evil-Merodach [Nebuchadnezzar's successor] became king of Babylon, he released Jehoiachin from prison on the twenty-seventh day of the twelfth month. He spoke kindly to him and gave him a seat of honor higher than those of the other kings who were with him in Babylon. So Jehoiachin put aside his prison clothes and for the rest of his life ate regularly at the king's table. Day by day the king gave Jehoiachin a regular allowance as long as he lived.
>
> 2 Kings 25:27-30

The records of these allowances referred to in the Bible were unearthed in excavations in Babylon in basement storerooms of the royal palace (in Staat-Liches Museum, East Berlin, Vorderas Abteilung; Babylon 28122 and 28126). These are known as the "ration tablets" and they record who received such "rations." In these, Jehoiachin is mentioned by name.

We also have confirmation of the Babylonian advance towards Judah in Nebuchadnezzar's first campaign. Among the ruins of Lachish were discovered a number of ostraca. Ostraca are broken pieces of earthenware called potsherds, which were used for writing on in ink. (The Lachish ostraca are in the Palestinian Archaeological Museum, Jerusalem.) These brief letters reveal the increasing tensions within the growing state of Judah and tie in well with the picture given in the Bible by the Book of Jeremiah the Prophet. In Ostracon VI, the princes are accused of "weakening our hands" (that is, discouraging the writers), which is the very phraseology used in the Bible by the Judean princes against Jeremiah. Also, the use of fire beacons for signaling is found in both Ostracon IV and Jeremiah 6:1, each using the same terminology.

These events took place around the year 600 B.C. Events we considered earlier in relation to the capture of Lachish by Sennacherib during the reign of Hezekiah were around the year 700 B.C.

We now take a jump back in time to the middle of the ninth century before Christ, that is, about 850 B.C. Most people have heard of Jezebel. She was the wife of Ahab, the king of the northern kingdom of Israel. Her wickedness has become so proverbial that we talk about someone as a "Jezebel." She urged her husband to have Naboth killed, simply because Ahab had expressed his liking for a piece of land owned by Naboth, who would not sell it. The Bible tells us also that she introduced into Israel the worship of her homeland, the Baal worship of Tyre. This led to the opposition of Elijah the Prophet and to the famous conflict on Mount Carmel between Elijah and the priests of Baal.

Here again one finds archaeological confirmations of what the Bible says. Take for example: "As for the other events of Ahab's reign, including all he did, the palace he built and inlaid with ivory, and the cities he fortified, are they not written in the book of the annals of the kings of Israel?" (1 Kings 22:39).

This is a very brief reference in the Bible to events which must have taken a long time: building projects which probably spanned decades. Archaeological excavations at the site of Samaria, the capital, reveal something of the former splendor of the royal citadel. Remnants of the "ivory house" were found and attracted special attention (Palestinian Archaeological Museum, Jerusalem). This appears to have been a treasure pavilion in which the walls and furnishings had been adorned with colored ivory work set with inlays giving a brilliant decorative effect. Numerous fragments of these were found. This ties in well, too, with the denunciations revealed by the prophet Amos:

> "I will tear down the winter house
>   along with the summer house;
> the houses adorned with ivory will be destroyed
>   and the mansions will be demolished,"
>   declares the LORD.
>
>   Amos 3:15

Other archaeological confirmation exists for the time of Ahab. Excavations at Hazor and Megiddo have given evidence of the extent of fortifications carried out by Ahab. At Megiddo, in particular, Ahab's works were very extensive, including a large series of stables formerly assigned to Solomon's time.

On the political front, Ahab had to contend with danger from the Aramaeans just to the north (present-day Syria). Ben-hadad is named in 1 Kings 20:1 as the king of Syria who besieged Samaria, Ahab's capital. Ben-hadad's existence is attested by a stela (a column with writing on it) which has been discovered with his name written on it (Melquart Stela, Aleppo Museum, Syria). Again, a detail of history given in the Bible is shown to be correct.

Consider, too, the threat in the entire Middle East from the power of Assyria. In 853 B.C. King Shalmaneser III of Assyria came west from the region of the Euphrates River, only to be successfully repulsed by a determined alliance of all the states in that area of the Battle of Qarqar. Shalmaneser's record gives details of the alliance. In these he includes Ahab, who he tells us put 2,000 chariots and 10,000 infantry into the battle. However, after Ahab's death, Samaria was no longer strong enough to retain control, and Moab under King Mesha declared its independence, as 2 Kings 3:4, 5 makes clear: "Now Mesha king of Moab raised sheep, and he had to supply the king of Israel with a hundred thousand lambs and with the wool of a hundred thousand rams. But after Ahab died, the king of Moab rebelled against the king of Israel." The famous Moabite (Mesha) Stone, now in the Louvre, bears an inscription which testifies to Mesha's reality and of his success in throwing off the yoke of Israel. This is an inscribed black basalt stela, about four feet high, two feet wide, and several inches thick.

Ahab's line did not last long and was brutally overthrown by a man called Jehu. As one walks toward the Assyrian section in the British Museum, one of the first exhibits to be seen is the famous Black Obelisk. This stands about six feet high and was discovered at Nimrud (Calah) near the Assyrian capital at Nineveh. It describes how King Shalmeneser III compelled Jehu to submit to his authority and to pay him tribute. Here one can see a representation of the kneeling figure of either Jehu or his envoy before the Assyrian king. The inscription tells of Jehu's submission: "The tribute of Jehu, son of Omri: I received from him silver, gold, a golden bowl, a golden vase with pointed bottom, golden tumblers, golden buckets, tin, a staff for a king and purukhti fruits."

Jehu is referred to by the Assyrian records as son of Omri, not because he was literally his son, but because he was on the throne which had been occupied previously by the house of Omri. This event took place about 841 B.C.

Putting them all together, these archaeological records show not only the existence historically of the people and events recorded in the Bible but the great accuracy of the details involved.

If we take another hundred-year step backwards in time, we come to King Solomon, son of David. On his death the Jewish kingdom was divided into two sections as a result of a civil revolt: Israel to the north with Jeroboam as king and Judah (as it was called subsequently) to the south under Rehoboam, Solomon's son. In both the Books of Kings and Chronicles in the Bible we read how during Rehoboam's reign: "Shishak king of Egypt attacked Jerusalem" (1 Kings 14:25; 2 Chronicles 12:2), and how Shishak stripped Rehoboam of the wealth accumulated by his able father, Solomon. The reality of this event is confirmed by archaeology to a remarkable degree.

Shishak subdued not only Rehoboam but Jeroboam as well. The proof of this comes first from a fragment in a victory monument erected by Shishak and discovered at Megiddo, a city in the land of Israel. So the Egyptian king's force swept northwards, subdued the two Jewish kings, and then erected a victory monument to that effect. Traces of the destruction have also been discovered in such cities as Hazor, Gezer, and Megiddo. These confirm what was written in Second Chronicles:

> . . . he [Shishak] captured the fortified cities of Judah and came as far as Jerusalem.

Then the prophet Shemaiah came to Rehoboam and to the leaders of Judah who had assembled in Jerusalem for fear of Shishak, and he said to them, "This is what the LORD says, 'You have abandoned me; therefore, I now abandon you to Shishak.' "

The leaders of Israel and the king humbled themselves and said, "The LORD is just."

When the LORD saw that they humbled themselves, this word of the LORD came to Shemaiah: "Since they have humbled themselves, I will not destroy them but will soon give them deliverance. My wrath will not be poured out on Jerusalem through Shishak. They will, however, become subject to him, so that they may learn the difference between serving me and serving the kings of other lands."

When Shishak king of Egypt attacked Jerusalem, he carried off the treasures of the temple of the LORD and the treasures of the royal palace. He took everything, including the gold shields Solomon had made.

2 Chronicles 12:4-9

Further confirmation comes from the huge victory scene engraved on Shishak's order at the Temple of Karnak in Egypt. The figure of the king is somewhat obscured, but he is clearly named and he is seen smiting Hebrew captives before the god Amon, and there are symbolic rows of names of conquered towns of Israel and Judah.

Solomon is remembered also for his great wealth. The Bible tells us:

The weight of the gold that Solomon received yearly was 666 talents, not including the revenues from merchants and traders and from all the Arabian kings and the governors of the land.

King Solomon made two hundred large shields of hammered gold; six hundred bekas of gold went into each shield. He also made three hundred small shields of hammered gold, with three minas of gold in each shield. The king put them in the Palace of the Forest of Lebanon.

1 Kings 10:14-17

This wealth that the Bible speaks of has been challenged. Surely, some have said, these figures are an exaggeration. Excavations, however, have confirmed enormous quantities of precious metals, owned and distributed by kings during this period. For example, Shishak's son Osorkon I (statuette of Osorkon I, Brooklyn Museum, New York), the one who stood to gain from the booty carried off from Rehoboam's capital, is reported to have made donations to his god Amon totaling 470 tons of precious metal, gold, and silver, during only the first four years of his reign. This, of course, is much more than Solomon's 666 talents which equals approximately twenty tons of gold per annum. We also have confirmation of the Bible's reference to Solomon's gold as coming from Ophir. The location of Ophir is still unknown, but an ostracon dated a little later than Solomon's time actually mentions that thirty shekels of gold had come from Ophir for Beth-horon.

So the story goes on. We have stopped at only a few incidents in the sweep back to the year 1000 B.C. What we hope has emerged from this is a sense of the historical reliability of the Bible's text. When the Bible refers to historical incidents, it is speaking about the same sort of "history" that historians examine elsewhere in other cultures and periods. This is borne out by the fact that some of the incidents, some of the individuals, and some of the places have been confirmed by archaeological discoveries. Of course, not all the incidents, individuals, and places have been confirmed, but the tide of archaeological discoveries in the past hundred years has swept away the possibility of a naive skepticism about the Bible's history. And what is particularly striking is that the tide has built up concerning the time before the year 1000 B.C. Our knowledge about the years 2500 B.C. to 1000 B.C. has been vastly increased through discoveries sometimes of whole libraries and even of hitherto unknown people and languages.

There was a time, for example, when the Hittite people, referred to in the early parts of the Bible, were treated as fictitious by critical scholars. Then came the discoveries after 1906 at Boghaz Koi (Boghaz-köy) which not only gave us the certainty of their existence but stacks of details from their own archives! [95]Two things should be mentioned about the time of Moses in Old Testament history.

First, consider the archaeological evidence that relates to the period. True, it is not of the same explicitness that we have found, say, in relation to the existence of Ahab or Jehu or Jehoiakim. We have no inscription from Egypt which refers to Moses being taken out of the bulrushes and removed from the waterproof basket his mother had made him. But this does not mean that the Book of Exodus is a fictitious account, as some critics have suggested. Some say it is simply an idealized reading-back into history by the Jews under the later monarchy. There is not reason why these "books of Moses," as they are called, should not be treated as history, just as we have been forced to treat the Books of Kings and Chronicles dating 500 years later.

There is ample evidence about the building projects of the Egyptian kings, and the evidence we have fits well with Exodus. There are scenes of brickmaking (for example, Theban Tomb 100 of Rekhmire). Contemporary parchments and papyri tell of production targets which had to be met. One speaks of a satisfied official report of his men as "making their quota of bricks daily" (Papyrus Anastasi III vso, p. 3, in the British Museum. Also Louvre Leather Roll in the Louvre, Paris, col ii, mentions quotes of bricks and "taskmasters"). Actual bricks found show signs of straw which had to be mixed in with the clay, just as Exodus says. This matter of bricks and straw is further affirmed by the record that one despairing official complained, "There are no men to make bricks nor straw in my area."

We know from contemporary discoveries that Semites were found at all levels of Egypt's cosmopolitan society (Brooklyn Museum, New York, no. 35.1446. Papyrus Brooklyn). There is nothing strange therefore about Joseph's becoming so important in the pharaoh's court.

The store cities of Pithom and Raamses (Rameses) mentioned in Exodus 1:11 are well known in Egyptian inscriptions. Raamses was actually the east-Delta capital, Pi-Ramses (near Goshen), where the Israelites lived (to the east of the Nile Delta). It had fertile tracts, an area where the Israelites would have had ample experience of agriculture. Thus, the reference to agriculture found in the law of Moses would not have been strange to the Israelites even though they were in the desert at the time the law was given. Certainly there is no reason to say, as some critics do, that these sections on agriculture were an indication of a reading-back from a later period when the Jews were settled in Canaan.

The form of the covenant made at Sinai has remarkable parallels with the covenant forms of other people at that time. (On *covenants* and *parties to a treaty*, see C. F. A. Schaeffer, Ugaritica III Louvre, Paris; the Code of Hammurabi in the Louvre; and Treaty Tablet from Boghaz Koi [i.e., Hittite] in Turkey, Museum of Archaeology in Istanbul.) The covenant form at Sinai resembles covenants from that period but *not* from later in the first millennium B.C. Thus, just as the forms of letter writing of the first century after Christ (the types of introductions and greetings) are reflected in the letters of the apostles in the New Testament, it is not surprising to find the covenant form of the second millennium before Christ reflected in what occurred at Mount Sinai. God has always spoken to people within the culture of their time, which does not mean that God's communication is limited by that culture. It is God's communication but within the forms appropriate to the time.

The Pentateuch tells us that Moses led the Israelites up the east side of the Dead Sea after their long stay in the desert. There they encountered the hostile kingdom of Moab. We have firsthand evidence for the existence of this kingdom of Moab—contrary to what has been said by critical scholars who have denied the existence of Moab at this time. It can be found in a war scene from a temple at Luxor (Al Uqṣor). This commemorates a victory by Ramses II over the Moabite nation at Batora (Luxor Temple, Egypt).

Also, the definite presence of the Israelites in west Palestine (Canaan) no later than the end of the thirteenth century B.C. is attested by a victory stela of Pharaoh Merenptah (son and successor of Ramses II) to commemorate his victory over Libya (Israel Stela. Cairo Museum, no. 34025). In it he mentions his previous success in Canaan against Aschalon, Gize, Yenom, and *Israel;* hence there can be no doubt the nation of Israel was in existence at the *latest* by this time of approximately 1220 B.C. This is not to say it could not have been earlier, but it cannot be later than this date.

⁹⁶We should take one last step back into the history of the Old Testament. In the previous note we looked first at the Dead Sea Scrolls, dating to around 100 B.C. Then we went back to the period of the Late Monarchy and looked first at the siege of Hezekiah in Jerusalem by Sennacherib in 701 B.C. and also at the last years of Judah down to about 600 B.C. Then we went further back to about 850 B.C., to Ahab and Jezebel, the ivory house, the Black Obelisk, the Moabite Stone and so on—then back again to about 950 B.C., to the time of Solomon and his son Rehoboam and the campaign by Shishak, the Egyptian pharaoh.

This should have built up in our minds a vivid impression of the historic reliability of the biblical text, including even the seemingly obscure details such as the ration tablets in Babylon. We saw, in other words, not only that the Bible gives us a marvelous world view that ties in with the nature of reality and answers the basic problems which philosophers have asked down through the centuries, but also that the Bible is completely reliable, *even on the historical level.*

The previous notes looked back to the time of Moses and Joshua, the escape from Egypt, and the settlement in Canaan. Now we will go back further—approximately 500 years before Moses—to the time of Abraham. We are now back as far as Genesis 12, near the beginning of the Bible.

Do we find that the narrative fades away to a never-never land of myths and legends? By no means. For we have to remind ourselves that although Genesis 12 deals with events a long time ago from our moment of history (about 2000

B.C. or a bit later), the civilized world was already not just old but ancient when Abram/Abraham left "Ur of the Chaldeans" (*see* Genesis 11:31).

Ur itself was excavated some fifty years ago. In the British Museum, for example, one can see the magnificent contents of a royal burial chamber from Ur. This includes a gold headdress still in position about the head of a queen who died in Ur about 2500 B.C. It has also been possible to reconstruct from archaeological remains what the streets and buildings must have been like at the time.

Like Ur, the rest of the world of the patriarchs (that is, of Abraham, Isaac, and Jacob) was firm reality. Such places as Haran, where Abraham went first, have been discovered. So has Shechem from this time, with its Canaanite stone walls, which are still standing, and its temple.

> He [Abram] took his wife Sarai, his nephew Lot, all the possessions they had accumulated and the people they had acquired in Haran, and they set out for the land of Canaan, and they arrived there.
>
> Abram traveled through the land as far as the site of the great tree of Moreh at Shechem. The Canaanites were then in the land, but the LORD appeared to Abram and said, "To your offspring I will give this land." So he built an altar there to the LORD, who had appeared to him.
>
> From there he went on toward the hills east of Bethel and pitched his tent, with Bethel on the west and Ai on the east. There he built an altar to the LORD and called on the name of the LORD. Then Abram set out and continued toward the Negev.
>
> Genesis 12:5-9

Haran and Shechem may be unfamiliar names to us but the Negev (or Negeb) is a name we have all read frequently in the news accounts of our own day.

Now we should turn to one of the most spectacular of modern archaeological discoveries, Ebla. While digging on an extensive mound forty-four miles south of Aleppo in Syria in 1974/75, an Italian archaeological expedition came across another of the vast libraries to which we referred earlier. A small room within the palace suddenly yielded up a thousand tablets and fragments, while another not far away a further fourteen thousand. There lay row upon row, just where they had fallen from the burning wooden shelves when the palace was destroyed about 2250 B.C.

What secrets did these tablets reveal? Without wishing to seem unnecessarily repetitive, we can say immediately that Ebla represents yet another discovery from the ancient past which does not make it harder for us to believe the Bible, but quite the opposite. And remember, these tablets date from well before the time of Abraham. The implications of this discovery will not be exhausted by even the turn of this century. The translation and publication of such a vast number of tablets will take years and years. It is important to understand that the information we now have from Ebla does not bear directly upon the Bible. As far as has been discovered, there is no certain reference to individuals mentioned in the Bible, though many names are similar, for example, Ishmael, Israel, and so forth. Biblical place names like Megiddo, Hazor, Lachish are also referred to. What *is* clear, however, is that certain individuals outside the Bible who previously had been considered fictitious by the critical scholars, simply because of their antiquity, are now quite definitely historic characters.

For example, the Assyrian King Tudiya (approximately 2500 B.C.) had already been known from the Assyrian king list composed about 1000 B.C. His name appeared at the head of the list, but his reality was dismissed by many scholars as "free invention, or a corruption." In fact, he was very much a real person and is known now from the Ebla records to have made a treaty with the king of Ebla. Thus, the genealogical tradition of the earlier parts of the Assyrian king list has been vindicated. It preserves faithfully, over a period of 1,500 years, the memory of real, early people who were Assyrian rulers. What we must learn from this is that when we find similar material in the Old Testament, such as the genealogical list in Genesis 7 or the patriarchal stories, we should be careful not to reject them out of hand, as the scholars have so often done. We must remember that these ancient cultures were just as capable of recording their histories as we are.

The most important aspect of the Ebla discoveries is undoubtedly their language. This has been found to be an ancient West-Semitic language to which such languages as Hebrew, Canaanite, Ugaritic, Aramaic, and Moabite are related. Thus we have now, for the first time, the whole "tradition" of West-Semitic language stretching over 2,500 years—something which was previously true only of Egyptian and Akkadian, to which Babylonian and Assyrian belong.

Up until quite recently, therefore, this meant that scholars could argue that many words which appeared in the Hebrew Old Testament were what they called "late." What they meant by this was that these words indicated a much later authorship than the time stated by the text itself. It would be as if one of us pretended to write a sixteenth-century book using such modern words as *automobile* and *computer*. In the case of the Pentateuch, for example, this was one of the arguments which led some scholars to suggest that it was not Moses who wrote these books, as the Bible says, but anonymous scribes from approximately 1,000 years later. The discoveries at Ebla have shown that many of these words were not late, but very early. Here is yet another example of a claimed "scientific" approach that merely reflects the philosophical prejudices of the scholars involved.

[97] A common assumption among liberal scholars is that because the Gospels are theologically motivated writings—which they are—they cannot also be historically accurate. In other words, because Luke, say (when he wrote the Book of Luke and the Book of Acts), was convinced of the deity of Christ, this influenced his work to the point where it ceased to be reliable as a historical account. The assumption that a writing cannot be both historical and theological is false.

The experience of the famous classical archaeologist Sir William Ramsay illustrates this well. When he began his pioneer work of exploration in Asia Minor, he accepted the view then current among the Tübingen scholars of his day that the Book of Acts was written long after the events in Paul's life and was therefore historically inaccurate. However, his travels and discoveries increasingly forced upon his mind a totally different picture, and he became convinced that Acts was minutely accurate in many details which could be checked.

What is even more interesting is the way "liberal" modern scholars today deal with Ramsay's discoveries and others like them. In *The New Testament: The History of the Investigations of Its Problems*, the German scholar Werner G.

Kümmel made no reference at all to Ramsay. This provoked a protest from British and American scholars, whereupon in a subsequent edition Kümmel responded. His response was revealing. He made it clear that it was his deliberate intention to leave Ramsay out of his work, since "Ramsay's apologetic analysis of archaeology [in other words, relating it to the New Testament in a positive way] signified no methodologically essential advance for New Testament research." This is a quite amazing assertion. Statements like these reveal the philosophic assumptions involved in much liberal scholarship.

A modern *classical* scholar, A. N. Sherwin-White, says about the Book of Acts: "For Acts the confirmation of historicity is overwhelming. . . . Any attempt to reject its basic historicity, even in matters of detail, must now appear absurd. Roman historians have long taken this for granted."

When we consider the pages of the New Testament, therefore, we must remember what it is we are looking at. The New Testament writers themselves make abundantly clear that they are giving an account of objectively true events.

[98]Acts is a fairly full account of Paul's journeys, starting in Pisidian Antioch and ending in Rome itself. The record is quite evidently that of an eyewitness of the events, in part at least. Throughout, however, it is the report of a meticulous historian. The narrative in the Book of Acts takes us back behind the missionary journeys to Paul's famous conversion on the Damascus Road, and back further through the Day of Pentecost to the time when Jesus finally left His disciples and ascended to be with the Father.

But we must understand that the story begins earlier still, for Acts is quite explicitly the second part of a continuous narrative by the same author, Luke, which reaches back to the birth of Jesus:

> In those days Caesar Augustus issued a decree that a census should be taken of the entire Roman world. (This was the first census that took place while Quirinius was governor of Syria.) And everyone went to his own town to register.
>
> So Joseph also went up from the town of Nazareth in Galilee to Judea, to Bethlehem the town of David, because he belonged to the house and line of David. He went there to register with Mary, who was pledged to be married to him and was expecting a child. While they were there, the time came for the baby to be born, and she gave birth to her firstborn, a son. She wrapped him in strips of cloth and placed him in a manger, because there was no room for them in the inn.
>
> Luke 2:1-7

In the opening sentences of his Gospel, Luke states his reason for writing:

> Many have undertaken to draw up an account of the things that have been fulfilled among us, just as they were handed down to us by those who from the first were eyewitnesses and servants of the word. Therefore, since I myself have carefully investigated everything from the beginning, it seemed good also to me to write an orderly account for you, most excellent Theophilus, so that you may know the certainty of the things you have been taught.
>
> Luke 1:1-4

In Luke and Acts, therefore, we have something which purports to be an adequate history, something which Theophilus (or anyone) can rely on as its pages are read. This is not the language of "myths and fables," and archeological discoveries serve only to confirm this.

For example, it is now known that Luke's references to the titles of officials encountered along the way are uniformly accurate. This was no mean achievement in those days, for they varied from place to place and from time to time in the same place. They were *proconsuls* in Corinth and Cyprus, *asiarchs* at Ephesus, *politarchs* at Thessalonica, and *protos* or "first man" in Malta. Back in Palestine, Luke was careful to give Herod Antipas the correct title of tetrarch of Galilee. And so on. The details are precise.

The mention of Pontius Pilate as Roman governor of Judea has been confirmed recently by an inscription discovered at Caesarea, which was the Roman capital of that part of the Roman Empire. Although Pilate's existence has been well known for the past 2,000 years by those who have read the Bible, now his governorship has been clearly attested outside the Bible.